James H. Brewer earned his Ph.D. in educational administration. His professional experience spans the fields of public education, higher education, banking, and private business. He is affiliated with Kelwynn, Inc., a training and development company.

J. Michael Ainsworth, an executive manager with Kelwynn, holds an MBA degree from Harvard University and has been an executive manager in creative marketing and in the areas of health care and video production.

George E. Wynne is also a Harvard Business School graduate. He has been a senior executive manager in the utility and banking industries, as well as in the military, and is now with Kelwynn, Inc.

Prentice-Hall International, Inc., *London*
Prentice Hall of Australia Pty. Limited, *Sydney*
Prentice-Hall Canada Inc., *Toronto*
Prentice-Hall of India Private Limited, *New Delhi*
Prentice-Hall of Japan, Inc., *Tokyo*
Prentice-Hall of Southeast Asia Pte. Ltd., *Singapore*
Whitehall Books Limited, *Wellington, New Zealand*
Editora Prentice-Hall do Brasil Ltda., *Rio de Janeiro*

POWER MANAGEMENT

James H. Brewer | J. Michael Ainsworth | George E. Wynne

KELWYNN

A SPECTRUM BOOK

Prentice-Hall, Inc., Englewood Cliffs, New Jersey 07632

Library of Congress Cataloging in Publication Data

Brewer, James H. (James Herman), (date)
  Power management.

  "A Spectrum Book."
  Includes index.
  1. Management. 2. Power (Social sciences)
I. Ainsworth, J. Michael. II. Wynne, George E.
III. Title.
HD38.B687 1984   658.4'09   83-19640
ISBN 0-13-687682-X
ISBN 0-13-687674-9 (pbk.)

This book is available at a special discount when ordered in bulk quantities. Contact Prentice-Hall, Inc., General Publishing Division, Special Sales, Englewood Cliffs, N.J. 07632.

10 9 8 7 6 5 4 3 2 1

ISBN 0-13-687682-X

ISBN 0-13-687674-9 {PBK.}

Editorial/production supervision by Chris McMorrow
Cover design by Hal Siegel
Manufacturing buyer: Pat Mahoney

Scattered quotations from Readings in Managerial Psychology, 2nd ed., ed. Harold J. Leavitt, © 1964, 1973 by the University of Chicago, are reprinted with permission of the University of Chicago Press, Chicago 60637.

Contents

Preface

Power is. It always has been a part of human relationships. It always will be. Power is an inescapable part of who we are and how we act. All organizations are structured formally and/or informally along the lines of definable power structure. The afternoon bridge club and the Soviet bureaucracy have one thing in common: a power structure. Someone sets the rules. Someone sets the time of actions. Someone defines the limits of acceptable behavior. Someone rewards success. Someone punishes those who violate the rules. All these actions are actions of power.

Power is the force by which the outcome of events is modified and shaped. People respond to power, either seeking its rewards or avoiding the unpleasantness of opposition. Because power may be used for self-seeking ends and because it has often been used in ruthless ways, people may view power as a coercive and negative force. However, power is neither good nor bad. Power is amoral. Power and the principles of power may be used for beneficial or malevolent ends. The judgment of its quality comes from the perceptions of its use and the outcomes of that use. The same use of power that rewards one group may deprive another. Determinations of good or evil will vary between those groups. Therefore, power itself should not be feared. Power should be studied so that it may be applied in ways that will generate the greatest benefit. This use of power is a key element in successful leadership.

The student of power should also realize that all power is limited. There is no one in any organization who is omnipotent. Conversely, there is no one who is powerless. Each of us has bases of power. Each of us has limitations. Knowing how to use our power most effectively and recognizing its limits are the key concepts in *Power Management*. By practicing these concepts, we can gain greater control over our lives and organizations.

This book is about power, the reality of it, and the management of it for effective leadership. We have made a great effort to avoid generalizations about power and its use. As a result of reading this book, you will understand how to find and use personal and position power. What is more, you will better understand yourself and how to develop the language of leadership.

Power Management will give you unique insights into how to use your own power cycle, how to use power motivation techniques, how to make your communications more powerful, and above all, how to develop a system of applying all the principles learned in the book. Only by reading all the contents sequentially will you be able to gain these insights.

Anyone who tries to influence another needs to read *Power Management*. Influencing others is a leadership process, and the essence of leadership is power. You will not be a successful leader without knowing how to manage power.

Power Management is the first book to structure the explanation of using power in simple and understandable steps. In addition, *Power Management* is the first book that develops a leadership language. When you finish the book, you will be able to use terms, symbols, and numbers that convey a world of information and save hours in decision making.

The objective of *Power Management* is to prepare you to understand and manage your power for effective and dynamic leadership. It will become clear to you how easy it is to increase your effectiveness in the home, business, department, or organization by applying the principles outlined in this book. You can start now increasing your personal and position power.

Power Management

1

Power Is

The most compelling reality that humanity faces is that, for better or worse, power will be used. It is not, nor has it ever been, a matter of whether but of how. This being the case, then, it becomes imperative that those who study power for the good of humanity outnumber those who study it for self-reward. However, as Michael Korda pointed out, "Now that sex is a subject that can be openly discussed, power seems to be the one dirty little human secret we have left to hide."[1]

Power is both exalted and condemned, praised and cursed, advocated and repelled. In more recent times, power has been condemned because of the thought that it dehumanizes individuals. The idea that one human uses or has power over another is repugnant to our modern society. Even Demosthenes, who lived before Christ, observed, "There is nothing, absolutely nothing which needs to be more carefully guarded against than that one man should be allowed to become more powerful than the people."[2]

The abuse of power attracts our attention, even holds a fascination for us. In a speech in 1771, Edmund Burke said, "The greater the powers, the more dangerous the abuse."[3] The army, police, intelligence agencies, and regulatory agencies all build power to repel power. Consequently, our usual perception of power is not a positive one and affords us no pleasure or reward of thought.

However, there is a need to understand how, at the worst,

people abuse power and how, for the better, power can be used for humanity. By studying both sides of power, we gain insight into its use. Francis Bacon (1561–1626) said, "Knowledge and human power are synonymous."[4] The individual, then, who does not understand power is unlearned.

Power is not a simple concept. There are as many definitions of power as there are authors, philosophers, theorists, psychologists, and so on. From the simple concept that power is one human being's influencing another to the more complex idea that power is life it-self, the meaning of power becomes indeed very complex. The Swiss poet Henri Frederic Amiel took this view, "Knowledge, love, power—there is the complete life."[5] If indeed knowledge as well as love is power, then the study of power truly becomes a complicated and complex study.

The more modern approach to the study of power involves the behavioral sciences. Motivation, communications, interpersonal relations, leadership, personal and position influence, and organizational systems are all areas which involve power. The concept of power can be studied only in relationship to other natural and human activities. The management of power can be comprehended best when it is merged into modern fields of behavioral sciences.

HISTORIC VIEW OF POWER

To understand the modern use of power, we must first have a historic perspective. The great philosophers tended to think of power as a life process. To them, the ability to do or the capacity to act was power. However, more has been written on the use of power in government than any other area. In 1735, Andrew Hamilton observed:

> We ought at the same time to be upon our guard against Power, wherever we apprehend that it may affect ourselves or our Fellow-Subjects . . . . Power may be justly compared to a great river which, while kept within its due bounds is both beautiful and useful; but when it overflows its banks, is then too impetuous to be stemmed, it bears down all before it and brings destruction and desolation wher-ever it goes. If this then is the nature of power, let us at least do our duty, and like wise men use our utmost care to support liberty, the only bulwark against lawless power, which in all ages has sacrificed to its wild lust and boundless ambition the blood of the best men that ever lived.[6]

To see power as a great river helps us gain a picture of how power can be used and abused in fields other than government. However, since human power is active in interpersonal and societal circumstances, government is thus a prime instrument for making power legitimate. Victor Cousin pointed this out in 1828:

> The right of government expresses the rights of all and each. It is the right of personal defense transferred to a public force, to the profit of common liberty.
>
> Government is not, then, a power distinct from and independent of society; it draws from society its whole force. It is not what it has seemed to two opposite schools of publicists,—to those who sacrifice society to government,—to those who consider government as the enemy of society. If government did not represent society, it would be only a material, illegitimate, and soon powerless force; and without government, society would be a war of all against all. Society makes the moral power of government, as government makes the security of society.[7]

What we learn from Cousin's observations is appropriate not only to government but also to interpersonal and organizational life. Authority and freedom are both functions of the legitimate use of power in the human experience. Authority gives us structure and order in our dealings, and freedom is expressed, by each in a personal way, through that order.

It is evident from a historical perspective that as John Adams said, "Power must never be trusted without a check."[8] If we learn anything from history, this should be it. The same is true between individuals and within organizations. An English poet said it this way, "Power will intoxicate the best hearts, as wine the stronger heads. No man is wise enough nor good enough to be trusted with unlimited power."[9]

The major concept we learn from the historic view of power is that humanity's freedom depends on every individual's involvement in power, not on that of only the few. Everyone's participation in the family, business, organization, or whatever makes us all powerful in the most positive sense.

DEFINING POWER

The Latin word for power is *posse*, which means *to be able*. This definition is very close to that of *strength*. Indeed, strength is a source of power, both muscular and moral. Consequently, there is an implication in this definition of the ability to use strength to control or accomplish some deed.

In another sense, power is the possession of a specific faculty such as hearing, seeing, or talking. A person with a talent possesses a specific power, for example, the talent of an artist. It is something that few others can master or perform. In addition, individuals may find certain powers related to personality types. The power to relate well to people can be a function of personality.

It is also true that power has a dimension of vigor or force implied in its meaning. One with great ability to act with force has extraordinary power. To force is to accomplish something against an obstacle, either human or natural. Although usually perceived to be negative, force as a part of power is good or bad depending on the situation.

One of the most common conceptions of power is that it involves the control, authority, or influence over others. In our modern social structure, to have power over others seems to be unacceptable. When we say that we have influence or authority over someone, it sounds much more acceptable. However, the concepts of power, authority, and influence are very closely related. In its most positive form, power is what holds a society together, allows it to grow, and enables it to serve its people.

In the same way that nature or a government can be a power, an individual can have great influence, force, or authority. A person with an organizational position has prescribed authority over others. In addition, the person who develops personal attributes can have immeasurable influence, or power, over people even without an organizational position. In the truest sense, anyone who uses an organizational position or personal power is a leader.

It is helpful when defining power also to understand the meaning of *powerlessness*. The opposite of power, powerlessness implies weak, impotent, and unable individuals, things, or organizations. However, the state of power or powerlessness is seldom static. There is always movement between the two. Consequently, power and powerlessness are relative terms and take meaning only when comparisons are made.

In this text, we define power as the force by which events, people, and organizations are changed. With this definition, we can understand that organizations, things, or people must, as a natural process, push against obstacles and make constant adjustments to the environment as needed. The use of force to make changes is the essence of power.

One other dimension of power, taken from mathematics, is that of the product of multiplying a quantity by itself. For instance, 32 is the fifth power of 2. When the positive use of power is made, it multiplies the social happiness of all. As David McClelland has pointed out, "The positive or socialized face of power is characterized by a concern for group goals, for finding those goals that will move men, for helping the group to formulate them, for taking initiative in providing means of achieving them, and for giving group members the feeling of competence they need to work hard for them."[10]

We have an obligation to study and use positive power for the betterment of humanity. Positive power takes many forms, and it is to our advantage to explore them. Unfortunately, we know too well the results of the negative use of power in the home, society, organization, and world.

TAKING POWER OUT OF THE CLOSET

The first step in the positive use of power is to take it out of the closet. As Martin and Sims have observed, "It is true, as many others have pointed out in different connections, that we in this country have an instinctive revulsion against the term 'power.'"[11] This is true, and as long as we refuse to take an honest and frank look at power, it will continue to be true.

We must remind ourselves, as the English writer Crossman once pointed out, "It is not power itself, but the legitimation of the lust for power which corrupts absolutely."[12] And George Bernard Shaw gave credence to the positive meaning of power by saying, "Power does not corrupt men; fools, however, if they get into a position of power, corrupt power."[13]

Power cannot corrupt if the human is not corrupt; power can be moral if the human is moral. The problem is getting moral mankind to recognize and use positive power. Yet even the term "positive power" raises fear in some. Some would think that any use of power is related to manipulation.

Another reason for the continued distrust of power is that writers about power cannot agree on terms and definitions. Take, for example, this excerpt from *Power and Innocence* by Rollo May, "Certainly force, the lowest common denominator of power, has been widely identified with power in America; it is the automatic first association with power of most people in this country. This is the chief reason power has been scorned and disparaged as a 'dirty word.'"[14]

Yet it is not force that should be scorned—only coercive force which is bad. Force in and of itself can be either good or bad. Positive force can be a counterforce against crime, discrimination, or violence and thus be a positive power. Consequently, an enemy to the positive use of power is simply the language we use. Inconsistent meanings and wrong connotations of words and terms drag us back into the darkness of the closet.

If power is to be studied, careful attention must be given to its related language. There will need to be some way to look at power in an unemotional, analytical process. Emotionally charged words such as *force, destruction, inferiority, superiority, competitive, manipulative,* and so on must be redefined or eliminated when used in the study of power. The truth is that a new set of code words or terms must be developed if the study of positive power is going to be effective.

SOURCES OF POWER

Power is manifested in our interdependence with others, and the sources of power spring from that human interaction. All of our wants and most of our needs express themselves only in our relationships to others. We are connected to others for our supply of food, clothing, housing, transportation, wealth, and so on. Our motives or desires move us toward our individual goals, but to reach these goals we need power over others either as individuals or collectively. While the few *sources* of human power are generated from our wants and needs, there are many *kinds* of power which are both positive and negative.

The intensity of the human behavior to satisfy wants and needs is called *motivation.* A complex web of power coalitions is formed by mankind to satisfy individual and collective wants and needs. This force of power is used to change relationships in all societies because human expectation is always changing.

Again, there is nothing inherently wrong with satisfying wants and needs, motivation, or using power. It is how they are used to serve self *and* society that makes the difference. As a general rule, power is bad when it serves the few and good when it serves the many. It is this fact that led to the establishment of governments, organizations, and businesses. Each of these finds a place in serving the wants and needs of a larger clientele or in protecting the many from the few. It is this economic and social system that is structured to guard against the abuse of power. Fairness in the marketplace, protection against crime, and fair reward for work are all part of the system that reflects the true source of human power, which is the satisfaction of our own wants and needs.

THE STRUGGLE FOR POWER

The struggle of the human being toward achieving goals is an individual learning process. Each person must experience the growth of moving from an inferior position to a more mature status. It was Alfred Adler, sometimes called the father of individual psychology, who pointed out that to be a human being means to possess a feeling of inferiority which constantly presses toward its own conquest. The paths to victory are as limitless as the chosen goals of perfection. The greater the feeling of inferiority that has been experienced, the more powerful the urge to conquest and the more violent the emotional agitation.[15]

In other words, individuals achieve only when they act to overcome powerlessness. If those acts are legitimate, then society benefits. This is a very important concept in the study of power. Again, true achievement is stimulated only when the human being strives to turn a weakness into a strength or moves from powerlessness to power.

In every new activity, the human being starts from an inferior position. Through learning, knowledge, and experience, the individual moves up the developmental levels toward superiority over the situation. Again, Adler points out, "The very stimulation growing from an uninterrupted feeling in inadequacy developed foresight and precaution in man, and caused his soul to develop to its present state, an organ of thinking, feeling, and acting."[16]

The struggle for power by the individual goes through several stages. First, a person must learn the basics of a process or activity. Knowing how, when, where, and other facts is fundamental to overcoming an inferior position. Second, an individual moves from learning the basics to communicating with others about why the activity is accomplished a certain way and learning to use skills for the community good.

Next, the individual progresses to a level where he or she is able to contribute to the decision-making process with others. At this level, the person begins to realize the social implications of positive power and shares responsibility for it.

Finally, when a person reaches the highest level of power, full independent maturity is attained. The individual is able to make responsible decisions for self and others. To this individual, power implies socially beneficial good rather than just personal gain.

Early in life, it is the family that serves as the place for learning the levels of power. A child needs an emotionally secure environment in which to learn and test basic skills. Interpersonal relationships are established in which power is expressed. The competitive nature of power shows up in sibling rivalry, and the nurturing side of power is evidenced in the loving and caring relationships that develop.

It is interesting that these same dimensions of individual power are present and expressed in organizations. Just as in the family, people within the organization will compete for the leader's attention, depend on nurture from a higher authority, and learn how to establish family-type relationships. In a real sense, this is what we call "office politics." And, as in a family, the larger the organization, the more potential there is for it to happen.

The human being is never completely satisfied in the struggle for power and, in fact, may sometimes regress in that struggle. The constant shift in the status of the individual hinders reaching a complete state of satisfaction and rest. Yet it is that state of dissatisfaction that creates growth and achievement.

The individual's struggle for personal power inevitably is confronted by another's struggle for power. As McClelland has said, "The negative or personal face of power is characterized by the dominance–submission mode: if I win, you lose."[17] This immature interpersonal exchange is found more often at the lower levels of personal power development. Immature, aggressive, and violent behavior springs more from powerlessness than from power. There is no need for such "I win, you lose" behavior when people are able to participate in power.

Harold Leavitt puts it this way:

> Power is often thought of pejoratively. We talk about 'power plays,' 'power-hungry people,' 'power politics,' and 'power tactics.' All of these have implications, if not of evil, at least of inequity or gamesmanship. All of them seem to stand in contrast to virtuous notions like 'fair play' and 'merit.' And yet it is obvious to any executive (or any parent for that matter) that if we weren't pretty sophisticated about power and its uses, we would be dead in the water. If most of us weren't pretty skillful power tacticians, neither the organization nor the family would survive for long. This is not to avoid or deny the huge ethical problems that center around the power question. But it does seem important to recognize from the start of this discussion, that power and influence are parts of our everyday life. While each of us must properly be continuously concerned about using power ethically and justly, to deny its central role in human relationships is nonsensical.[18]

It is also true that people compare themselves to others and the results are either a feeling of inferiority or superiority. The concept we have of ourselves is based on the continuous comparison of how we are doing in relation to others. It is because of this comparison, then, that the ever-shifting process of compensation starts again.

This compensation results in relationships of dominance and submission. Some individuals feel superior only when they can dominate others. Although we find this at the lower end of personal power development maturity, most of us see dominance and submission as a general function of power. Yet in reality it can be an elusive concept.

If the ultimate objective of an individual's behavior is to reach some personal goal, submission or dominance may, depending on the situation, achieve that goal. For instance, our submission to a doctor for the cure of an illness helps us reach our goal of being well. We would also submit ourselves to the direction of a leader we perceived could help us gain greater rewards. In a sense, however, the effective leader submits to the wishes of the followers in order to retain the leadership position.

Students of power will need to analyze relationships of people, groups, organizations, and governments in terms of mutual benefit and not just submission or dominance. It could be that what seems to be an obvious "I win, you lose" situation is in reality beneficial to both parties, much like the example of submission to the doctor in which both parties win.

THE POSITIVE MANAGEMENT OF POWER

If power is a force by which events, people, and organizations are changed, we must somehow make sure that it is used for mutual benefit. Only when we study and understand power can we make progress in this regard. When the reality of power is ignored or even condemned, society suffers from its negative use.

The positive management of power takes place when

1. we recognize the existence of power,
2. we see the concept of power as having a positive side,
3. we learn how to analyze and use positive power,
4. we use communication, motivation, leadership, and organizations to enhance everyone's power, and
5. we understand and use the developmental process in helping ourselves and others reach a mature use of power.

In summary, we are not naive about power or the misuse of it. The reason that the use of negative power is so abundant, even by good people, is that it is allowed to fill the void left by the lack of use of positive power. As this trend reverses, the growth into the positive use of power must of necessity include not only self-interest but also the good of humanity. This must be true in every family, organization, business, and government.

It is easy to be cynical about power. As Michael Korda says, "No matter who you are, the basic truth is that your interests are nobody else's concern, your gain is inevitably someone else's loss, your failure someone else's victory."[19] Korda seems to draw the conclusion that people should use power as a means of fulfilling their own desires, that is, power for personal reward.

While it is agreed that the source of power is our desire to fulfill our wants and needs, we are all bound together in the effort. We are interdependent, and our struggle for power should always include mutual interests. We should reject the idea that one person's failure is another's victory. Life is not that simple, and we are unalterably entwined in each other's destiny. What increases one person's positive power inevitably increases that of all.

NOTES

1. Michael Korda, *Power! How To Get It, How To Use It* (New York, N.Y.: Random House, Inc., 1975), p. 8.
2. Demosthenes (380–322 B.C.), Oration XIX, cited by George Seldes, ed., *The Great Quotations* (Secaucus, N.J.: Castle Books, Inc., 1977), pp. 201, 202.
3. Edmund Burke, Speech, Middlesex Election, 1771, cited by George Seldes, ed., *The Great Quotations* (Secaucus, N.J.: Castle Books, Inc., 1977), p. 127.
4. Francis Bacon, (1561-1626), English essayist, cited by George Seldes, ed., *The Great Quotations* (Secaucus, N.J.: Castle Books, Inc., 1977), p. 73.
5. Henri Frederic Amiel, (1821-1881), Swiss poet, cited by George Seldes, ed., *The Great Quotations* (Secaucus, N.J.: Castle Books, Inc., 1977), p. 55.
6. Andrew Hamilton, Defense of Peter Zenger, 1735, cited by George Seldes, ed., *The Great Quotations* (Secaucus, N.J.: Castle Books, Inc., 1977), p. 296.
8. John Adams, To Jefferson, Feb. 2, 1816, cited by George Seldes, ed., *The Great Quotations* (Secaucus, N.J.: Castle Books, Inc., 1977), p. 44.
9. Charles Caleb Colton (1780--1832), English poet, cited by George Seldes, ed., *The Great Quotations* (Secaucus, N.J.: Castle Books, Inc., 1977), p. 168.
10. David C. McClelland, *Power—The Inner Experience* (New York: N.Y.: Irvington Publishing, Inc., a division of John Wiley Sons, 1975), p. 72
11. Norman H. Martin and John Howard Sims, "Power Tactics," in *Readings in Managerial Psychology*, 2nd ed., ed. Harold J. Leavitt (Chicago, Ill.: University of Chicago Press, 1973), p. 272.
12. Richard Howard Stafford Crossman, English writer, *New Statesman and Nation*, April 21, 1951, cited by George Seldes, ed., *The Great Quotations* (Secaucus, N.J.: Castle Books, Inc., 1977), pp. 186, 187.
13. George Bernard Shaw (1856-1950), Irish dramatist and critic, in Stephen

Winstien, *Days with Bernard Shaw*, cited by George Seldes, ed., *The Great Quotations* (Secaucus, N.J.: Castle Books, Inc., 1977), p. 632.

14. Rollo May, *Power and Innocence* (New York, N.Y.: Dell Publishing Co., Inc., 1972), p. 100.

15. Alfred Adler, *The Individual Psychology of Alfred Adler*, ed. Prof. Heinz L. Amsbacher and Rowena R. Amsbacher (Simm des Lebens, 1933).

16. Alfred Adler, *Understanding Human Nature*, trans. W. B. Wolfe (Garden City, N.J.: Garden City Publishing Co., 1927), pp. 29–30.

17. McClelland, *Power–The Inner Experience*, p. 85.

18. Harold J. Leavitt, *Managerial Psychology*, 4th ed. (Chicago, Ill.: The University of Chicago Press, 1978), pp. 136-37.

19. Korda, *Power*, p. 4.

2
Power
In Organizations

Power is and always has been a part of human experience, and the exercise of power is a function of the interactions between people. This "economy of power" is a reflection of our interdependence and of our need for what others can do for us. Power does not exist for human beings unless it becomes active in a collective system.

From the beginning of our existence on earth, human beings have banded together. This was originally necessary because, compared to other animals, human beings are weak and physically inferior. This early herd instinct allowed for the development of organizations for self-protection and for the acquisition of food and shelter.

Although we may think otherwise, there is nothing new about an age of specialization. The primitive cultures had members who specialized in specific functions in the organization. There were those who hunted, those who made shelter, clothing, and weapons, and so on. Depending on the value of their specific skills, individuals were given power. Consequently, even the most primitive organizations had power structures.

It is also true that individual human beings were always reaching for new or different goals. These goals could be accomplished much more efficiently and in less time if others helped. One individual would convince another that a goal was worth the effort and that an organized division of labor would speed its completion. Today's organizations are, of course, much more complex. The leadership skills needed are much more involved than those used in hunting for food. Even the organization of the home is more complex.

An organization consists of parts or components that work together in a systematic way. The human organization is formed into a group by members to work toward some end. In our society, the modern organization is formed to fulfill the wants and needs of others and, at the same time, meet certain desires of its own members.

THE ORGANIZATION AS A SYSTEM

The organization that does not use the collective power of its members to overcome survival problems will soon fall from existence. Organizations, like people, must develop ways to overcome weaknesses. Consequently, we must understand how the organization responds to internal and external powers that affect its performance. Leaders must recognize how organizational systems work.

Leadership theories often fail because, either in inception or implementation of a plan, they do not recognize the nature of systematic organizations. All modern organizations are formal or informal systems. A system is by definition a collection of interdependent components, each bearing a unique and fundamental relationship to the whole. The removal or alteration of any major component of the system will significantly change or perhaps destroy the entire organization. Consequently, a leader must make judgments in the context of a system because decisions are not made in a void. The effect of a single action is influenced by other decisions made by other decision makers.

Organizations are power-based systems. In all systems there is a force that holds the system together and defines its limits (Figure 2-1). In a physical system, such as the solar system, that power is gravity. In human organizations, the force is most often a political power.

Regardless of the nature of the organization, there is a decision-making process that is influenced by numerous demands. The decisions made in the organization create new demands and new changes. This is the nature of a political organization, and this is the power base behind effective leadership. As Zaleznik has pointed out:

"The main job of organizational life, whether it concerns developing a new political pyramid, making new appointments to executive positions, or undergoing management succession at top levels, is to bring talented individuals into location for the legitimate uses of power."[1]

FIGURE 2-1. Organizational System.

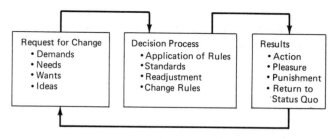

ORGANIZATIONAL CHANGE

In the organizational system, change depends on how the decision makers perceive the severity of the demands. Leaders in the organization constantly adjust and change priorities based on the request for change. The need for change can be a function of outside or inside forces. Moreover, those outside forces or powers can be people, things, or events.

Change takes place on two levels—for the organization and for its members. If an organization does not react to the needs, demands, and wants of new circumstances, it fails. One dramatic example of new circumstances seen in the last few years is the idea that employees need to become more involved in decisions affecting production. Consider this situation: The plant workers wear blue Nissan uniforms. Office workers go outside at 7:30 each morning for Japanese calisthenics. The Japanese-type training focuses on teamwork and family. Yet the plant is Nissan Motor Manufacturing Corporation, U.S.A., in Smyrna, Tennessee.

The company spent $63 million to train workers at Smyrna with another $7.3 million provided by the State of Tennessee. The assembly line training is not only in one or two specialized skills but also includes interpersonal relations, equipment operation, and machinery maintenance. Nissan managers say that the multiskilled worker tends to be more productive and happier than traditional assembly line workers.

Employees report that management makes them feel important by listening to what they have to say. This is because the plant has participatory management designed around the Quality Circle concept. Frequent meetings between workers and supervisors keep the lines of communication open. Each assembly line worker has the power to stop and correct product flaws and to help solve production problems.

This Japanese management system so widely discussed today revolves around workers as team players. Americans, on the other hand, have traditionally been individualistic. There are, of course, other differences. The common thread in Japanese life is intimacy, and this caring, support, and unselfishness of the Japanese people is found at the work site. In the United States, personal feelings usually have no place at work.

There are, however, formal organizations in the United States that have always had a high degree of participation from the membership. In fact, one well-respected American institution has been recognized, even by the courts, to allow its professional staff to be considered part of management. In other words, the professional staff can make organizational changes, interview staff additions, set employment standards, and revise client standards if they desire. Consequently, the professional staff operates as management and, to a large degree, the administrative leadership is at the mercy of the professional committee structure. This, of course, is the American college and university system. Until recently, there were few outside demands which affected the internal operation of these institutions. However, with the prospect of a declining client population, major changes are beginning to be made. For example, many colleges now provide continuing education for individuals in business, education, and government. Whether or not the American college system in part or in whole can successfully respond to the wants and needs of society as a whole remains to be seen.

The leader must also recognize some of the problems found in any organization and some causes of the power plays people use to resist change. Part of the responsibility of any leader is to overcome these unproductive behaviors on the part of followers. However, the followers themselves may not understand these behaviors and how they affect productivity.

CHANGING FOLLOWERS

Often when leaders attempt to cause change in their organization, they are met with great opposition from members. Behavioral change is often the most painful change process with which people deal. It requires commitment and the acknowledgment that change is desirable. Yet, there are many reasons why people are reluctant to change. Here are some of the major reasons.

Fear of Change

Change requires risk, and that creates anxiety and stress, which almost all people work hard to avoid. Our fear is that the outcome of anything new will be worse than our present circumstances. In believing this, we discount our abilities. To overcome this fear, we must confront the change head-on and take well-planned risks as they are required.

Defeatist Belief Systems

Some people refuse to acknowledge their ability to effect meaningful change and work hard to create justifications for this belief. Blaming irresponsible behavior on personality traits is a common justification: "I just have a hot temper, and there is nothing I can do about it!" This is a denial of the personal power to control the situation. Such a denial is a major cause of pessimism and unmotivated behavior.

Lack of Skills and Resources

When leaders have decided to make a change, followers must have the skills necessary to effect that change. Followers must know how to do that which is required. Asking people to make a change, convincing them that change can be made, and then leaving them without the necessary skills and resources to implement that change is a sure way to create nonproductive behavior, raise the resistance level of followers, and support defeatist belief systems. When we implement change, we should identify skill deficits and find opportunities to train followers affected by the change. We should identify the necessary resources and be sure that appropriate methods of applying those resources are clear.

Hope

Hope is usually considered a virtue, but it can be a major drawback to effective change. In this sense, hope implies the belief that our fate is in the hands of forces outside our control. We believe that once something hoped for happens that everything will be all right and we will live happily ever after. Yet there are no fairy tales in real life, and wishing does not make things happen; doing makes things happen. We should accept the reality of life and work to make our own worlds what we want them to be.

The outcome for positive change of followers depends on the leaders efforts, energy, and enthusiasm. However, when negative power is used in an organization to facilitate change, leaders must recognize that the following may happen:

1. There may be a disruption to the day-to-day routine.
2. A great deal of fear may be generated.
3. Participation by other lower leaders will be limiting.
4. Lower leaders will feel their authority reduced.
5. Loyalty to the leader and organization will be reduced.

When the leader uses negative power, followers use individual power plays to deal with the stress. When there is disruption in the work situation, some people resort to power plays in which someone will win and someone will lose. Even though considerable effort may be expended in overcoming the barriers to organizational change, change often still does not come about in a positive way. In fact, it may seem that each new attempt to improve the system just makes matters worse. Why does this happen?

Each attempt to alter the environment puts established individual relationships in jeopardy. Each new action threatens the old power bases upon which desirable behaviors were previously defined. To protect established positions of power, people in organizations actively engage in a number of behavioral power plays. These power plays are designed to minimize the impact of change and strengthen the position of the individual player.

These are interactions for individual power, not activities that further the objectives of the organization. Consequently, these power plays will disrupt the implementation of organizational systems that focus on overall organizational change or that attempt to alter individual behavior in ways that diminish the power of the players.

POWER PLAYS

Leader knowledge of these power plays and their impact on organizations is critical to the implementation of effective organizational systems. These are several of the power plays used by followers.

The Vulture

The player waits for someone to make a mistake, or in some cases, arranges for another person to fail in a task. When this happens, the player moves in for the kill. The player feels superior and maintains power by reminding others of their faults.

The Perfectionist

This player points out only errors in the work of others. In reviewing pages of data, the perfectionist will comment only on the misspelled word or the misplaced comma. The perfectionist tries to make others feel inadequate.

The Double Dipper

In this power play, the player puts the other party in a position such that any action that person takes will work against them. This is the power play of applying a double standard. An example is the leader who demands aggressive action by subordinates but finds such behavior unacceptable in female employees.

The Con Artist

In this power play, the player offers a false reward, such as a bonus for a certain level of performance. Once someone has qualified for the reward, the rules are changed and the promised reward is not provided.

The "I'm Better"

This is a favorite of people who feel self-righteous. Rather than socializing with other employees, they sit in the office avoiding contact with the outside world and minimize the luxury of their surroundings. In this way, demands of others are deflected. How can more be requested from a person content with so little?

The "I'm Excused"

This is a cop-out to avoid accomplishment. Physical or social handicaps are used as an excuse for effort. Failure to accomplish is blamed on a deprived background or other reason—failure that should be excused through the mercy of the leader. This person may be well-qualified for the position but lets an excuse stand in the way of performance.

The Put Downer

This is perhaps the most common power play between staff and line functions. It is a way to put people down without their being fully aware that it is happening. While giving the appearance of cooperation, the "yes, but . . ." player will reject any advice given. No solution is acceptable.

The Complainer

This power play brings problem solving to a halt. It directs energy that should be applied to problem solving into a session in which players simply complain about the state of affairs. This is a power play of gossip in which people and departments spend considerable time and effort reviewing the awful things other persons or groups are doing.

The Spectator

In this power play, one person creates dissension between two other players. After building the dissension to the point of argument, the first player sits back and watches the other two waste their energy in confrontation.

All organizations have people, and people make power plays because of threats to their values, personality, or power base. The leader's job is to reduce the effect of the power plays as much as possible, knowing that he or she may not or cannot eliminate them all. Even small power plays, however, can sometimes bring productivity to a halt if not checked.

BEHAVIORAL DRIVERS

There are a number of basic behavioral principles we have learned through the course of our lives that greatly influence our overall behavior. These principles are called "drivers." Drivers can be good in the sense that they give structure to our lives. However, uncontrolled drivers can modify our behavior in negative ways and reduce our personal power. Following are some of the most common drivers.

Win!

Winning at all costs is a behavioral driver within individuals that may reduce the desire to cooperate. When the urge to win is uncontrolled it may drive away others who are needed to help with productivity.

Be Perfect!

Much stress is generated within individuals who feel they must be perfect. When the desire for perfection reduces or stops productivity, it becomes negative.

Hurry Up!

Most individuals are not equipped to do a good job in a hurry; nevertheless, in our society it is almost a truism that fast is good. This idea not only hurts quality, but it also actually slows down productivity because so many tasks must be done again.

One of the problems resulting from power plays and behavioral drivers in any organization is that the leaders or other members may have a false perception created about the players. Power plays are expressions of frustration. While the frustration of organizational change does affect productivity, the leader must be careful about making personnel evaluations based on that type of behavior.

"He's got an attitude problem!" "Sally would be a good worker if she just had the right attitude." These statements are typical of judgments made in every type of organization. Attitude is a concept often discussed in terms of effectiveness. Although a good attitude is often related to effectiveness, a good attitude should never be accepted without question as a hallmark of a productive worker. "The winning attitude" is a concept taken from sports competition to be the basis for many judgments we make about people in the work environment.

No one would question that attitude is an important element of success. Whole industries have been founded on the power of positive thinking. However, judgments about attitude are invariably subjective in nature. Consequently, they and they alone simply cannot be the basis for sound leadership decisions.

In any organization the purpose of leadership is the accomplishment of goals and objectives. Doing is important, and attitude is a factor only to the extent that it assists in the performance of job accomplishment. Behavior, not attitude, is the benchmark by which evaluations of subordinate performance must be made.

POLITICS IN ORGANIZATIONS

In a formal sense, any organization has just so much room at the top. Often described as a pyramid, the common organizational structure has fewer and fewer decision makers toward the top of the organizational chart. Consequently, a two-way conflict develops, either openly or covertly, between organizational leaders. There is a constant struggle either to get to the top or get the attention of the top leader.

The conflicting ambitions of the members of an organization will either be channeled for the common good or for self-interest. The member must decide whether it is more beneficial to stay in the organization or resign. In the final analysis, the member who finds himself or herself with a weak power base will be the most likely to leave.

However, the wise organizational member realizes that while there may be a scarcity of organizational positions, there is no such limit on personal power. The individual who possesses skills, expertise, motivation, and intelligence will always be able to build a personal power base. Yet the trick is for the individual to use those qualities for the good of the organization and its members. A person who intends to build a personal power base must not, therefore, be perceived by others as being self-serving, for there cannot be any observable conflict of interest between the individual and the organization's goals.

To say, for example, that an organization is formed only to sell a product is too simplistic. Many other political goals must be recognized, such as the aspirations of the members, the salaries, a meaningful workplace, a sense of belonging for members, and so on. In other words, organizations seldom have just one reason for being. The exercise of power in an organization boils down to each member's influencing the system and its people to fill as many personal wants and needs as possible. This influencing process is the foundation for politics in the organization.

BUILDING POWERFUL ORGANIZATIONS

The "chemical composition" of any organization is determined by environmental pressures, personalities of its members, hidden and stated goals, and leadership dynamics. In addition, organizations and families serve much the same purpose in filling the emotional needs of their members.

The happiness of the members in an organization will to a large degree be determined by the compatibility of each individual's personality type and the characteristics of the organization. It is easy to recognize that all organizations are not alike. However, we have only recently begun to recognize that while ability, skill, motivation, intelligence, and experience are important factors in performance, personality type may have more of an effect on production than any other factor.

Leaders who desire to build powerful organizations must consider that

1. humans are interdependent upon each other,

2. an "economy of power" exists in any organization,

3. the organization is a system which must respond to the demands of external and internal environments,

4. change creates power plays among the organization's workers,

5. members of any powerful organization must participate in the power of that organization,

6. participation by members must be carefully planned,

7. the delegation of power to followers must be based on the circumstances surrounding the task assignment,

8. motivational tools, communication, and interpersonal relations should be studied and calculated to meet the specific needs of individual members, and

9. leadership in the organization should be based on a rational, structured, and unemotional decision-making process.

In summary, an organization is a means to an end. It serves the wants and needs of a clientele as well as its own members. Within any organization, power is expressed through the interactions of its members. It is when this power is used in positive and constructive ways that individuals and organizations grow. The organization that does not respond to inside and outside demands (that is, move from an inferior to superior posture) will not survive.

The competition for resources in primitive societies created power struggles between tribes or bands of human beings. In the process, members in each band became more interdependent. This is no less true today than it was then. Leaders in organizations must recognize the interdependence of the members and draw upon that power. The greater the mutual benefits the organization holds for leaders and followers alike, the greater the motivation will be to work for and foster organizational goals.

NOTES

1. Abraham Zaleznik, "Power and Politics in Organizational Life," *Readings in Managerial Psychology*, 2nd ed., ed. Harold J. Leavitt (Chicago, Ill.: University of Chicago Press, 1973), p. 299.

3

The Importance of Power in Leadership

It is time for the re-emergence of positive and constructive leadership in America. We have lost much of our influence not only in world political affairs but also in economics and business. If this country is to regain its place of world leadership, the period of self-examination of the 1960's and 1970's must be followed by strong determination in the 1980's. The leadership of this new effort will certainly not use the same techniques as in the past but will be no less dynamic.

Because the people of the United States are so diverse, there is a need for a unique leadership and management system tailored specifically for America. It should utilize methods and techniques that are based on a strong sense of purpose. This new system will of necessity rely on pragmatic yet forceful leadership. Leadership that understands and uses influence over events and people with the enthusiastic affirmation and consent of followers will be the most successful.

Leadership is an influencing process. It has, in the broadest sense, taken place when one person has changed behavior because of another's actions. In a way, a baby who cries to be fed can influence the behavior of its mother. The power of influence over the mother can be called a basic type of leadership. Consequently, anyone who changes the behavior of another is a leader. It is this broad concept of leadership that will be discussed in this text.

DEFINING LEADERSHIP

In order to adequately understand and define leadership, let us first quickly review some of its aspects which have been discussed in the past. Throughout history, humanity has selected a few individuals to make decisions that affect the many. As Ralph Waldo Emerson has observed, "Mankind have, in all ages, attached themselves to a few persons, who, either by the quality of that idea they embodied, or by the largeness of their reception, were entitled to the position of leaders and law-givers."[1]

The process of leading involves the influencing or inducing of others to behave in a desired manner. But how does a leader influence others? When defining leadership, we are forced to look at the qualities of an individual. What characteristics does an effective leader have? The traits that make a leader are as elusive today as they were when Champ Clark wrote in 1899,

> What constitutes the quality of leadership, Mr. Speaker? You do not know. I do not know. None of us knows. No man can tell.
>
> Talent, genius, learning, courage, eloquence, greatness in many fields we may define with something approximating exactness; but who can inform us as to the constituent elements of leadership? We all recognize the leader the moment we behold him, but what entitles him to that distinction is and perhaps must forever remain one of the unsolved mysteries of psychology.
>
> Talent, even genius, does not make a man a leader, for some men of the profoundest talents, others of the most dazzling genius, have been servile followers and have debased their rich gifts from God to the flattery of despots.
>
> Courage is not synonymous with the quality of leadership, though necessary to it, for some of the bravest soldiers that ever met Death upon the battlefield and defied him to his face were amazingly lacking in that regard.
>
> Learning does not render a man a leader, for some of the greatest scholars of whom history tells were wholly without influence over their fellow-men. Eloquence does not make a leader, for some of the world's greatest orators, among them Cicero, have been the veriest cravens; and no craven can lead men.

> Indeed, eloquence, learning, talents, genius, courage, all combined do not make a leader.
>
> But whatever the quality is, people recognize it instinctively, and inevitably follow the man who possesses it.[2]

How can we study leadership if we don't know what it is? There are at least four factors that have a great impact on effective leadership. They are personality, circumstances, types of behavior, and power. However, we cannot define leadership only in terms of influence. We need to remember also that leadership is a broader concept than management. While management works toward achieving organizational goals, leadership actively seeks to influence events and people to reach all types of goals.

As discussed earlier, the use of power is a fact of leadership and cannot effectively be ignored. Abraham Zalenznik has pointed out that leadership is the "exercise of power."[3] If this is true, then power is the essence of leadership. And as Merrell says:

> To influence events and people, a leader must have power, which is a social and psychological leverage with people and institutions. The sources of power include professional and technical expertise, formal positions of authority, the legal rights of office, a knowledge of procedures, and the control of scarce resources and services.
>
> Power is also affected by interpersonal skills—the ability to persuade, motivate, and organize. Access to influential people in an organization enhances power, as does access to vital information that would be helpful in carrying out organizational goals. The capacity to dominate and intimidate others when necessary and the ability to resist domination are also important.
>
> The capacity to lead is one thing, but the courage to act decisively to make use of power is what finally counts. Power allows leaders to move the organization in a meaningful direction toward the achievement of key objectives.[4]

Consequently, we can define leadership power as the demonstrated or perceived ability of an individual to change events, people, and organizations. Leadership must be used or demonstrated in order to be called leadership. An unsuccessful attempt to change events, people, and organizations is not an act of leadership. Having the potential for leadership may be in some way comforting, but only when an individual's ability to lead is active can we evaluate real leadership power.

Power, again, need not be a negative concept. As McClelland says, power must have a positive face, too. After all, people cannot help influencing one another; organizations cannot function without some kind of authority relationships.[5] The question remains, however, one of how power will be used.

THE TWO BASIC KINDS OF LEADERSHIP POWER

Several factors determine the power base of any leader. In his observation of the business world, Zalenznik says that managers' and executives' power bases consist of three elements:

1. The quality of formal authority vested in his position relative to other positions.

2. The authority vested in his expertise and reputation for competence (a factor weighted by how important the expertise is for the growth areas of the corporation as against the historically stable areas of its business).

3. The attractiveness of his personality to others (a combination of respect for him as well as liking, although these two sources of attraction are often in conflict).[6]

Although researchers have identified many kinds of individual power, most fall within two categories: personal and organizational. Each serves a different function yet both are necessary for effective leadership.

Personal power is influence ability the individual possesses apart from title or other formal office. It can be said that the individual brings it to the job or organization. Personality, physique, communication style, and other personal factors create personal power.

On the other hand, organizational power is influence ability the individual possesses because of a title or other formal office. The title or office is given by others in the organization. Because of title or office, the individual can exercise power over others. Other types of power do exist and will be discussed later relating to how the leader can develop personal and position power within the organization.

It should be pointed out, however, that perception has a great deal to do with leadership power. Although an individual has, or seems to have, personal or organizational power, the degree to which he or she actually possesses that power is a matter of each follower's perception. For instance, there are those who, by their appearance, look like leaders. We tend to give these individuals influence beyond their organizational rank.

LEADERSHIP THEORIES

Anyone who is a serious student of leadership development must understand the three leadership theories that have been pervasive over this century. This understanding should serve as an evaluation tool when exploring leadership power and leadership training and development programs.

Leadership researchers in the past have asked the following questions:

1. Is leadership effectiveness determined by a set of *traits* in the human personality?
2. Are there observable *leader behaviors* that determine effective leadership?
3. What does the particular environment, *contingency*, or situation have to do with effective leadership?

Trait Theory

Trait leadership theory began around the turn of the century and was studied and researched for almost fifty years. Its basic premise was that if one could identify leadership traits, it would be possible to transfer them to non-leaders. The hope was that leaders could be made—not just born. Many attempts were made to identify and transfer personality traits in order to create leaders. Characteristics such as those pointed out by Champ Clark—courage, eloquence, learning—were once thought to be universal to all great leaders. Schools, academies, colleges, military institutes, and leadership training programs were established to develop desired leadership traits in students.

However, after almost a half century of trait research, no agreement was reached on the question of common leadership traits. Although this is true, there is still a popular belief that personality plays an important part in leadership.

Behavior Theory

Leadership researchers were interested in making leadership studies more scientific and more suitable to empirical research. Leadership behavior seemed to be observable and could be classified. In 1918, for example, Bogerdus classified leadership behavior into four types: (1) autocratic, (2) executive, (3) democratic, and (4) reflective.[7]

In a major study at Ohio State University in 1945, researchers found leader behavior could be reduced to two functions: (1) initiating structure and (2) worker consideration. In addition, a graphic model was produced that represented four mixes of these leadership functions. This model was to serve as the basis for other leadership models that followed.

In time, such terms as autocratic, bureaucratic, diplomatic, democratic, and laissez-faire became familiar. Each term conveyed a specific style of leadership behavior. Students of leadership examined the pros and cons of each, and democratic behavior was most often identified as the best style. However, in 1958, Schmidt and Tannenbaum placed leadership styles on a continuum ranging from higher-leader authority to high-subordinate freedom.[8] A fuller discussion of these concepts will come later in this chapter.

Contingency Theory

From the early studies of leadership, it was noted that someone who was an effective leader in one situation might not be an effective leader in another. Leader effectiveness seemed contingent upon the circumstances or environment. Fred Fiedler (1967) is most often given credit for the major contribution to the area of contingency leadership studies.[9]

Fiedler research is at odds with those who feel that there is one "best" or "right" leadership style. Both camps, however, use the Ohio State University Model as the basis for their theories.

NEW MODELS

> Much leadership and management training today reflects vague or confused theoretical foundations, resulting in somewhat aimless training efforts. The seasoned eye can usually detect the implied theoretical base (or often several of them) underlying a particular training design and its published agenda. Frequently the program design and its parts are drawn, with no one seemingly aware of it, from fragments of theory buried in three pervasive theories of leadership dominating this century: trait, behavior, and contingency theories.[10]

Because there are no absolutes in human behavior, there are none in leadership. However, discarding years of leadership research would be foolish. Leadership development must use the tools of *all three* theories to become truly useful. It is evident from the research that leadership depends on the individual personalities of the leaders and followers, the leadership style or behavior being used, and the circumstances (contingencies) around a given task. Let us look at some of the major leadership models of the recent past in order to gain a foundation for later discussion.

McGregor's X & Y Theory

In his book *The Human Side of Enterprise*, Douglas McGregor describes two perceptions of people that managers have. Theory X assumes that people are inherently bad and find work distasteful. Theory Y, on the other hand, assumes that people see work as natural as play. The conventional view (Theory X), says McGregor, is that man works as little as possible, is inherently self-centered, resists change, and is not very bright. Conventional organization structures, leadership, policies, and procedures are organized around these assumptions.

On the other hand, the new theory of management (Theory Y), as described by McGregor, is that the "essential task of management is to arrange organizational conditions and methods of operation so that people can achieve their own goals best by directing their own efforts toward organizational objectives."[11]

McGregor speaks of management behavior such as "hard" or "strong" and "soft" or "weak." He also points out that there are difficulties in each type of behavior. However, we must note that McGregor recognized different styles of leader behavior even though he advocated only one—Theory Y.

McGregor assumed that being directed, manipulated, and controlled in organizations was all bad and that workers needed to be guided by self-control and self-direction. We now know that certain types of personalities want to be directed and controlled, and feel very uncomfortable providing self-direction. We have also begun to understand that at times leadership is effective only when it is in a directing or controlling mode.

In addition, McGregor assumed that when higher level needs were provided for in the workplace, productivity would go up. While this may be true in some situations, it is not in others. McGregor's theories do not explain the variables at work in the modern organization. His model attempts to describe the managerial environment but offers little direction in ways to alter and improve that environment.

Tannenbaum and Schmidt's Model

Tannenbaum and Schmidt constructed a leadership model that uses a continuum from authoritarian to democratic. They described how leaders could mix authority and subordinate freedom.

They said that their new model became necessary when evidence began to challenge the efficiency of highly directive leadership, and increasing attention was paid to their model of the continuum that indicates different mixes of leadership styles and behaviors.

According to Tannenbaum and Schmidt, there were "Forces in the Manager," "Forces in the Subordinates," and "Forces in the Situation," that dictated the selection of the appropriate leadership style. Selection of style, then, was a matter of personal variables, subordinate expectations, and environmental pressures.[12]

The Ohio State University Leadership Model

Leadership studies at Ohio State University and elsewhere found that leadership behavior had two dimensions: (1) the initiating of structure and (2) worker consideration. These two dimensions were mutually supportive to varying degrees. A graphic model was constructed to depict four combinations of consideration and initiating structure. The four quadrants suggested different mixes of the two dimensions.

The initiating of structure was behavior related to the work itself. The leader was finding ways to accomplish the task. On the other hand, worker consideration was behavior related to human relationship. The leader was finding ways to increase social contact, enhance trust, and so on (Figure 3-1).[13]

FIGURE 3-1. Ohio State Model.

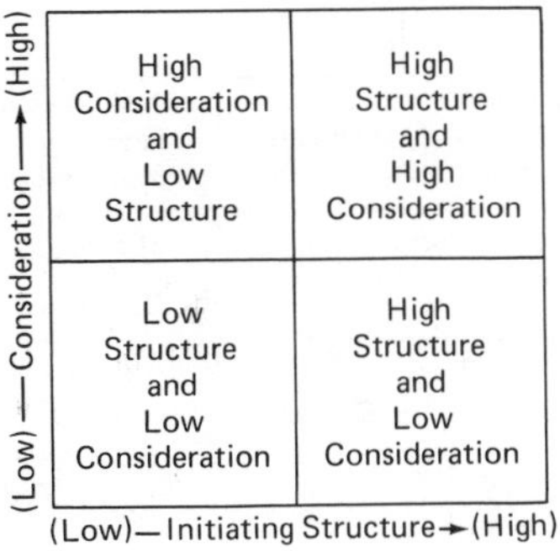

	(High)	
Consideration →	High Consideration and Low Structure	High Structure and High Consideration
(Low)	Low Structure and Low Consideration	High Structure and Low Consideration

(Low)— Initiating Structure → (High)

The Ohio State studies gave structure to the types of leadership behaviors and served to focus attention on the different leader styles

Blake and Mouton's Managerial Grid Model

Blake and Mouton say that there is one best way to manage in their theory of managerial leadership. To them, the 9,9 approach in their Managerial Grid Model "is acknowledged by managers as the soundest way to achieve excellence."[14] The 9,9 in the upper right corner of the grid shows the integration of task concern for production and of human concern for people (Figure 3-2).

FIGURE 3-2. Managerial Grid Model.

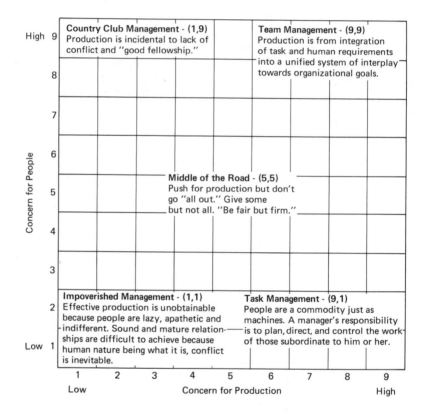

While Blake and Mouton expanded the Ohio State Model into the grid, they used similar terms like "concern for production" and "concern for people." Some critics of the managerial grid argue that concern is not a behavior but rather an attitudinal dimension. While this may be true, Blake and Mouton clearly describe five leadership styles or behaviors in the grid. In fact, the grid authors say a leader's actual behavior and conduct can be predicted from knowledge of how he or she thinks about achieving production with and through people.[15]

The Managerial Grid Theory notes that two aspects of management, task relationship and personal relationships, may coexist in varying degrees. This variance makes possible different combinations of leadership styles and different levels of task and people awareness. However, grid proponents contend that there is only one best style—the Team Manager.

The insistence that there is one best style of management ignores the vast complexity of modern organizations. Environmental factors are ignored in the attempt to impose an all-inclusive panacea. However, environmental conditions do affect behavior in organizations and must be considered in choosing a leadership style.

Hersey and Blanchard's Situational Leadership Model

Hersey and Blanchard recognize in their Situational Leadership Model that different styles of leadership depend on the situation and the maturity of the follower. The Situational Leadership Model (Figure 3-3) is based upon the leader's task and relationship behavior (á

FIGURE 3-3. Situational Leadership Model.

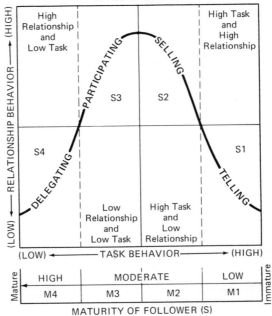

la Ohio State Model) which is dependent on the maturity of the follower on a specific task. It is the task-specific maturity level, then, that indicates to the leader which style of leadership to use.

Hersey and Blanchard also gave descriptive terms to each quadrant: Telling, Selling, Participating, and Delegating. The terms indicate a type of leader behavior based on the "willingness and ability" of the follower to do the task. Consequently, the two major considerations of Hersey and Blanchard's leadership model are the (1) leadership behavior which is based on (2) the maturity if the follower. "Situation" in the model refers only to the ability and willingness of the follower.[16]

Situational theories contend that there is no one best style of management. In situational management, the best style depends on two factors: (1) the specific task, and (2) maturity of subordinate. As the task changes and/or the maturity of the subordinate changes, then the appropriate style of management must change.

The contention that there are a number of best styles is more appropriate to modern organizations than those advocated by previous theories. However, once again, this model fails to consider the complete range of variables involved in leadership decision making. Most importantly, the theory ignores the personality characteristics of subordinates not related to task function or job maturity.

Again, the "situation" in the title of the model refers to the maturity of the subordinate. A full analysis of the leader's position, while discussed, is not a part of the decision-making process of the model.

Our understanding of leadership has been built upon the research, theories, and concepts developed over this century. Each new model builds upon the old. The review of these leadership theories in this chapter will serve to help us understand the new Power Management Leadership Model presented later in this book.

It is clear from the research that leadership is an influencing process. The degree to which the leader is successful in that process depends on power. There are levels of influence, degrees of power, and, consequently, different probabilities for leader success. It is also clear that the probability for success depends on the effective use of personality, specific leader behaviors, and circumstances in more powerful ways.

LEADERSHIP AND MANAGEMENT

If power is the essence of leadership, leadership is the essence of management. Management in an organization has been defined as getting things done through people. Yet today's manager is dependent on many other power forces in the work environment. As Kotter points out,

> A manager is more at the mercy of superiors, subordinates, peers in other parts of the organization, subordinates of peers, outside suppliers, customers, competitors, unions, regulating agencies—the list could go on and on.[17]

Because of these factors, the manager must recognize once again that leadership in managment is vital. In working with such a diverse set of forces, the manager needs personal and position power in order to survive. Many managers are promoted from technical positions in which they were high performers. However, unless they understand the leadership role and how to influence effective production in others, they will fail.

Effective management is as much knowing when to give power away as it is knowing when to keep it. That is, delegation is not an easy process and takes an understanding of the developmental process of followers. For instance, a manager should analyze the specific task to be assigned a follower before making the assignment. Otherwise the follower may be unable to accomplish the task and performance will be poor.

The point is that managers need to understand the leadership process and how to increase their position and personal power. This will take study and use of effective communications, motivational tools, various leadership styles, position analysis, and other proven leadership techniques. Leadership cannot be divorced from management.

In the final analysis, all management theories can be judged by one standard: Did the theory make the organization better? Regardless of its theoretical value, a management system must assist managers in accomplishing their goals and objectives. How can a management system do this?

An effective management system must recognize that there are three basic components to organizational accomplishment: (1) the work to be accomplished, (2) the resources to accomplish that work, and (3) the personal characteristics of the people who will use those resources in the accomplishment of the task. Unfortunately, previous systems have failed to recognize the interdependence of these three elements. Too often, undue stress has been placed on managers by the contention that failure to accomplish is due to a deficiency in personal style. Effective management and leadership must deal with more than style. It must recognize all the elements of accomplishment and the multitude of subelements in the system.

POSITIVE LEADERSHIP

If leadership is an influencing process, it is also a dependent process. No leadership takes place without followers. The leader who thinks otherwise will be surprised to find that although there is a line of authority, and there should be, followers have power upon which leaders depend. Mechanic puts it this way;

> Within organizations one makes others dependent upon him by controlling access to information, persons, and instrumentalities, which I shall define as follows:
>
> A. Information includes knowledge of the organization, knowledge about persons, knowledge of the norms, procedures, techniques, and so forth.
>
> B. Persons include anyone within the organization or anyone outside the organization upon whom the organization is in some way dependent.
>
> C. Instrumentalities include any aspect of the physical plant of the organization or its resources (equipment, machines, money, and so on).
>
> Power is a function not only of the extent to which a person controls information, persons, and instrumentalities, but also of the importance of the various attributes he controls.[18]

The first step to positive leadership is to determine who has what kind of power in the organization. Who will the leader be dependent on? Then the major task of the leader becomes one of forming positive power systems with those individuals. A positive power system is an interpersonal relationship built upon the maintenance or enhancement of both power bases. This concept is more fully discussed in Chapter 10.

There has been a concept in this country that the leader is not effective unless his or her leadership approach is antagonistic to followers, that followers are somehow to be whipped into shape, psychologically or otherwise. The idea of using followers as a power source is foreign to some leaders.

However, it is just as dangerous to conclude that letting followers participate in organizational affairs (that is, to gain personal power) in and of itself will increase productivity. In fact, when inappropriately used, participation may be counterproductive. The key becomes for the leader to know when to ask for participation and when not to. As stated before, it is as much knowing when to give power away as it is knowing when to keep it.

Power can shift suddenly from leader to follower. That is, the leader may suddenly find himself or herself very dependent on the follower for the success of the organization. For example, when there is an electrical power outage in a community, the human power shifts to a few expert linemen who have the knowledge to restore the service. In a nearby office building, there may be a top executive, a group of managers, even the mayor of the city, who are all at the mercy of the one person who can restore power to the thousands. Even the nonfunctional red light on the street has the potential for causing death. We are all dependent on each other, even in the leader-follower relationship.

Consequently, the leader who desires to lead in a positive and effective way should recognize that

1. leadership involves power,
2. power is more productive when it increases the power bases of both leader and follower,
3. followers have power that can be developed,
4. there are two kinds of leadership power—personal and position,
5. leadership models serve only as a guide to effective leadership,
6. personality, circumstances, leader behavior, and power affect productive leadership, and
7. power is the essence of leadership.

The task now is for the leader to build a personal system of power that will be productive over the short and long terms. This includes improving powers of communication, motivation, leadership behavior, decision making, and interpersonal relations. In addition, the managment of power will be most rewarding when put into a systematic vision of a plan of action.

The question is not simply one of whether or not to use power; it is, "How can we make better and more effective use of power?" In our modern society, we must come down on the side of positive power. We should have no illusions about negative, dehumanizing power—it exists and will always exist. Yet, we should firmly believe that there is a better way and that is positive power which leads us into productivity for true mutual benefit.

NOTES

1. Ralph Waldo Emerson, "Uses of Great Men," delivered in 1850, The World's Best Orations, Vol. V, ed. David J. Brewer (Akron, Ohio: The Werner Company, 1899), pp. 2020-21.
2. Champ Clark, "The Courage of Leadership," The World's Best Orations, Vol. III, ed. David J. Brewer (Akron, Ohio: The Werner Company, 1899), pp.1209-10.

3. Abraham Zaleznik, "Power and Politics in Organizational Life," *Readings in Managerial Psychology*, 2nd ed., ed. Harold J. Leavitt (Chicago, Ill.: University of Chicago Press, 1973), p. 281.

4. V. Dallas Merrell, "Working On Your Leadership Skills," *Supervisory Managment*, June 1981 (New York, N.Y.: AMACOM, a division of American Management Associations, 1981), p. 39. Reprinted by permission of the publisher, ©1981 by AMACOM. All rights reserved.

5. David McClelland, *Power–The Inner Experience* (New York, N.Y.: Irvington Publishing, Inc., 1975), p. 42.

6. Abraham Zaleznik, "Power and Politics in Organizational Life," in *Readings in Managerial Psychology*, 2nd ed., ed. Harold J. Leavitt (Chicago, Ill.: University of Chicago Press, 1973), p. 284.

7. E. S. Bogerdus, *Essentials of Social Psychology*, (Los Angeles: Jesse Ray Miller, 1918).

8. Robert Tannenbaum and Warren H. Schmidt, "How to Choose a Leadership Pattern," *Harvard Business Review*, March–April 1958, pp. 95-101.

9. Fred Fiedler, *A Theory of Leadership Effectiveness* (New York, N.Y.: McGraw-Hill Book Company, 1967).

10. James Owens, "A Reappraisal of Leadership Theory and Training," *Personnel Adminstrator*, Nov. 1981, p. 75. Reprinted from *Personnel Administrator*, copyright 1981, The American Society For Personnel Adminstration, 30 Park Drive, Berea, OH 44017, $30 per year.

11. Douglas McGregor, *The Human Side of Enterprise* (New York, N.Y.: McGraw-Hill Book Company, 1960). See also *The Management Review*, Nov. 1975, pp. 22-28, 88-92.

12. Tannenbaum, *Harvard Business Review*, 1958.

13. Ohio State University, Bureau of Business Research, 1975.

14. Robert R. Blake and Jane Srygley Mouton, "An Overview of the Grid," *Training and Development Journal*, May 1975, p. 32.

15. Ibid.

16. Paul Hersey and Kenneth H. Blanchard, *Management of Organizational Behavior: Utilizing Human Resources*, 4th ed. (Englewood Cliffs, N.J.: Prentice-Hall, Inc., 1982), pp. 152-55. ©1982. Reprinted by permission of Prentice-Hall, Inc., Englewood Cliffs, N.J.

17. John P. Kotter, *Power in Management* (New York, N.Y.: AMACOM, a division of American Management Associations, 1979), p. 10.

18. David Mechanic, "Sources of Power of Lower Participants in Complex Organizations," *Readings in Managerial Psychology*, 2nd ed., ed. by Harold J. Leavitt (Chicago, Ill.: University of Chicago Press, 1973), p.333.

4

Position Power

The more traditional organizational definition of *position* would include terms such as *office, post, rank, appointment, job, job slot,* or *incumbent*. These terms can be limiting. In this text, *position* will be referred to as *the circumstance or situation relative to the leader and follower and to the task to be accomplished*. In other words, position is the location, place, or circumstance of a person at a given moment. For instance, if Joe is a supervisor in a machine shop, that is his organizational position. His staff, resources, time schedule, and task to be accomplished are all elements in his position.

THEORIES ON CIRCUMSTANCES

Researchers turned to the study of the leadership situation when the study of leadership traits proved inadequate. As early as 1935, Pigors suggested that leadership be examined in terms of the situation.[1] In more recent times, Fiedler's model of contingency leadership was developed with the idea that the leader's behavior was contingent on the circumstances. He also suggested in his model which leadership style was most appropriate in a given situation.[2]

As can be seen, current leadership research has taken us far beyond McGregor's X and Y Theory, authoritarian versus permissive, and other traditional concepts. Leadership depends on many factors such as authority, the experience and ability of the followers, the complexity of the task, and a wide range of human personality factors. To think otherwise would be simplistic. However, Blake and Mouton, in their theory of management leadership, say that there is one best way to manage. They ignore the various factors of position. To them the 9,9 approach in their Managerial Grid Model "is acknowledged by managers as the soundest way to achieve excellence." The 9,9 "Team Manager" is one who increases production with "the integration of task and human requirements into a unified system of interplay towards organizational goals."[3] No other styles of leadership are recognized as productive regardless of the environment or personalities of the followers.

Hersey and Blanchard, on the other hand, do recognize in their Situational Leadership Theory that different styles of leadership depend on the "maturity" of the follower. This theory is based upon leader "task and relationship behavior," which is dependent on the maturity of the follower on a specific task.[4] It is the task's specific maturity level, then, that indicates to the leaders which style of leadership to use. The Hersey/Blanchard theory also ignores the personality dimensions of both the leader and the follower. As Beck says,

> While proponents of Situational Leadership make an attempt to look at the leader/follower transaction through more of a Fred Fiedler-inspired "follower" viewpoint, they miss an opportunity to push out of their behavioral constraints by examining why a particular person is "unable" to do the work or is "unwilling" to do so. To simply fix on those behaviors without asking why the follower is responding the way he or she is, places one in the position of using a formalized "cookie-cutter" in four shapes of S. Two people may be located in the M^2 group, within the continuum of both task and relationship dimensions, but may be quite different in their value systems.[5]

The term "situational leadership" may also be misleading as it is used in the Hersey-Blanchard model. The emphasis in their model is on the "leader/follower" relationship, and the leadership style to be used is based on the task-relevant maturity of the follower. Thus, in the Hersey/Blanchard model itself, all other situational factors are essentially discarded. It may be more appropriate to call their model a "leader/follower maturity relationship model."[6]

What is needed by the leader is a greater understanding of the major factors that make up the total situation or circumstances at a given time in the organization. Each of these factors could be critical to increasing or decreasing the position power of the leader. Let us say that Susan is a manager in a retail store. Her first task is to survey the circumstances of the organization and, more specifically, the tasks to be accomplished. What if Susan had an ample number of salespeople but no merchandise, or plenty of merchandise but no one who knew the prices? Susan has to analyze all of the circumstances, not just the maturity of her followers.

POSITION POWER

Amitai Etzioni defined position power as the ability to induce others to do a task because of position in the organization.[7] In this text, this type of power is referred to as *organizational power*. Position power will be defined by the authors as all power elements found in the total organizational circumstance or situation. In addition, it should be understood that position power elements can be used in the organization by the leader as well as by the followers. For instance, there are times when a follower knows more about the actual performance of a task than the leader. The follower has in this instance more position power than does the leader.

A power element is any major factor that has an effect upon the performance of a task. For instance, the availability of resources has a great deal to do with productivity. The follower cannot be responsible for lack of resources to do the job, and the lack of productivity in that case would be a problem for the leader to solve. However, if adequate resources are available for the task and production is still low, the leader must analyze other possible causes.

The major power elements in any organization include the following:

1. The degree of uncertainty in the environment.
2. The complexity of the tasks to be performed.
3. The ability and training of the followers.
4. The amount of information accessible to the follower.
5. The amount of resources available.
6. The time available to complete the task.
7. The motivation of the followers.
8. The personalities of the individuals involved.

The mere fact that we analyze and think about these factors in our position helps us to gain a greater perspective of the organization. In addition, as we will explore later, the information we receive from this analysis will help us determine the leadership approach we should take in solving organizational problems and making assignments. For example, let us say that Bob has two employees—one new and one experienced. He intends to give the same assignment to both. Will his approach be the same? What if one follower had the resources available to finish the task and the other did not? Would he still use the same approach?

Before moving on to a discussion of each of the power elements, there is an assumption here that we, as leaders, have the authority to exercise some control. When we have that ability to act upon our decisions within certain bounds, we have organizational authority. When we have organizational authority, we strive to turn weaknesses into strengths within our unit, department, or organization. For instance, if Mary has all of the resources, staff, motivations, and so on at her disposal to accomplish an assigned task but no authority to put it into action, she has no chance for success in leadership. Power is an influence that has strength.

POWER ELEMENTS

Productivity is movement toward achieving organizational goals. The three critical factors in the productivity process are the leader, the task, and the follower. What does the leader want done? Is the leader effectively communicating the task assignment to the follower? Can the specific task be accomplished under the circumstances? As an example, Bert notes that the lawn needs mowing. He communicates the task assignment to his son in such a way that the son is motivated to mow the lawn. However, since it has begun to rain, it is impossible for Bert's son to carry out the assignment.

In analyzing the power elements to follow, one must remember that we are trying to gain insight into our overall position power. Much valuable information will be gained from the followers themselves, and again, it should be remembered that they, like the leaders, also have position power. Since Bert's son has become an expert at mowing lawns, he suggests to his father that the neighbors' lawn mower be borrowed because it is not affected by wet grass. The knowledge of the follower served as a type of position power in this instance.

Environment

The things, conditions, or influences surrounding the leader and follower make up the environment. While the terms *circumstance, situation,* and *contingency* are sometimes used when describing the total organizational environment, the authors see it as only one power element of the organizational picture. Outside pressures, internal climate, and kind of organization all contribute to the environment. A police department, for instance, is quite different from an insurance company. The environmental pressures are different for each type of organization. The police department must react quickly to what, in some instances, can be a life or death matter, while the insurance company has a more stable day-to-day environment. On the other hand, insurance sales people using highly persuasive sales techniques must be able to relate to and interact with people.

The leader can reach a better understanding of the environment by determining the major characteristics of the organization. Four types of organizational environments/units can be identified:

A/C (Active/Competitive). The active/competitive type of organization or unit is characterized by reacting to much external ambiguity and changing conditions and is oriented to short-term results. Leaders in this type of organization must be able to cope with an ever-changing internal environment that calls for continuous, short-range problem-solving skills. Many times the leadership role in this organization is one of crisis management or emergency work. This organizational type is usually found to have highly competitive and/or risk-oriented conditions and activities. The police department or units within its organization must deal with crises or emergencies. Yet, there are many other highly competitive organizations in business whose survival depends on quickly changing to new technology that would be in this category. Another example is in trucking. A truck driver is in a different location every day, is independent, makes quick decisions, and is in a highly competitive operation.

P/I (Persuasive/Interactive). The persuasive/interactive organizations are characterized by their dealings with people and the selling of ideas. These organizations are dependent upon strong interpersonal relations. Leaders in this type of organization must be able to deal with and motivate others through skillful persuasion. Many times the leadership role in the P/I type of organization is one of participating, meeting, talking, and team planning. This type of organization is usually related to high people-interactive conditions and activities. When an organization such as an insurance company is highly dependent upon sales, it is a persuasive/interactive organization. If no one talks to prospective clients, makes a policy sale, or maintains customer satisfaction, an insurance company will not last long. Consequently, many meetings are held to motivate organizational members, and there are constant discussions on sales projections and goals.

W/S (Willing/Steady). The willing/steady type of organization is characterized by its concentration on routine, day-to-day work which needs follow-up. Leaders in this role must be able to follow a steady schedule, have an accommodating manner, and supervise specialized activities. Many times this organization is one of counseling, housekeeping, or servicing others. The W/S organization is usually associated with highly stable, routine conditions and activities. For example, many government regulatory agencies are W/S organizations. Keeping records, performing routine daily tasks, and answering citizens' inquiries are typical of their activities. Moreover, some of the skills needed by the workers become very specialized. Information stored on computers will demand well-qualified computer operators.

P/S (Precise/Systematic). The precise/systematic type of organization is characterized by compliance to standards and quality control and is dependent on following regulations. Leaders in this organization must be able to deal with precise, rule-oriented situations. Many times the P/S organization is one of processing, analyzing, organizing, and systematizing. This organization is usually found in highly organized and quality-demanding conditions and activities. An example is a company that manufactures computers. They must be built with precision and high-quality materials. Another example is an accountant who is judged by the quality of output, precision of analysis, organization, and compliance to standards.

No organization or department is purely one type, yet most organizational environments tend to fit into one of the categories. Another way of determining the environment is to ask, "The major activities of the majority of people in this organization or department involve... ?" Figure 4-1 is a listing of the characteristics which make up each of the four organizational categories. Remember that organizations may have several departments or divisions, each with different characteristics.

What we are trying to determine before any decisions are made is the nature of the beast. Is the environment simply reflecting the kind of organization it is supposed to be? Many leaders have made mistakes in their judgments and decisions about changes in the organization because they do not understand the environmental characteristics of their own organization.

For instance, giving customer relations training to assembly line workers (in a precise/systematic organization) would not be the best use of the available training budget. In the same way, giving salespeople (in a persuasive/interactive organization) volumes of regulations, paperwork, and standards to be responsible for may have diminishing returns.

FIGURE 4-1. Categories of Characteristics.

A/C (Active/Competitive)	P/I (Persuasive/Interactive)	W/S (Willing/Steady)	P/S (Precise/Systematic)
Variety of tasks	Contacting others	Staying in one place for client	Low risk
Solving problems	Motivating others	Concentrating on specific tasks	Adhering to procedures
Frequent changes	Speaking to others	Routine	Controlling quality
Directing others	Giving demonstrations	Counseling others	Proofing
Making quick decisions	Helping others	Using specialized skill	Following directions
Creating new ways of doing things	Selling ideas	Being patient with others	Putting things in order
Taking risk at times	Communicating	Listening to others	Evaluating others' work
Dealing with conflict	Team planning	Controlling information	Verifying
Working on short projects	Meeting with others	Being accommodating to others	Complying
Starting new projects	Performing before others	Working overtime	Being precise
Competing with others	Influencing others	Showing kindness to others	Keeping standards
Directing followers	Convincing others	Being patient with others	Recording information
Being open and direct with others	Mixing with others	Calming others	Making calculations
Getting quick results	Inspiring others	Doing skilled work	Arranging details
Working independently	Talking to others	Supporting organizational teamwork	Implementing prescribed work
Innovating	Interviewing others	Serving others	Analyzing procedures

The leader should ask several questions in determining the stability of the organization or departmental environment:

1. What are the natural characteristics of the organization?
2. What are the inside or outside forces that are upsetting those natural characteristics?
3. Are decisions about changing the environment based on logical assumptions or are they a reflection of the personality traits of the leader?
4. In terms of the specific task to be accomplished, what degree of certainty or uncertainty does the follower have to endure?

The "Position Analysis" to be discussed later calls for the leader to make a judgment about the environment. The greatest amount of good is gained when the analysis is specific as to task and follower. This is to say that the leader needs to look at the environment in light of a specific task and not generalize about all assignments being made in the total organization.

Task

Another power element to consider in the leader's position is the specific task to be accomplished. Is the task complex or simple? While these are relative terms, the question should be, "Is the specific task complex or simple to the follower who is assigned to do it?" If a task is complex to the follower, it does not necessarily mean that he or she is untrained or does not have the intelligence or ability to accomplish the task. While those factors may be present, it may simply be that the leader needs to spend time with the follower directing or developing greater understanding about the task.

Many times we assume too much in making task assignments and leave the follower out on a limb. For example, asking a subordinate to complete a task with many different components will necessitate directions and explanations from the leader. Let's say that Judy has been in the organization for some time and is well trained and informed in the skills she uses. Sally, her boss, assigns her a task with several new components and steps never used by Judy. She has the skills and training, but the procedure and arrangement of the task will take further explanation from Sally. Several questions the leader should ask in determining task complexity are as follows:

1. Is this task different from other routine tasks? Why?
2. What is the length of time needed to accomplish that task? (May indicate complexity.)
3. Are new skills or training needed for this task?
4. Does the task involve new things, data, or people?

Again, we need to do our analysis in regard to a specific task and specific follower. While one task may be complex to a follower, another may be simple.

Training

In analyzing the power element of training, what we want to do is ask, "Is this person trained or untrained to do this specific task?" It is not a simple question because nonperformance of a task is not necessarily a training problem. Robert I. Mager puts it this way, "People don't do things for zillions of the darnedest reasons, leading to all sorts of problems. And when there are problems—caused by differences between what people do and what someone wants them to do—the common solutions are to inform or exhort, or both."[8]

Tasks involve things, data, and people. In our analysis of the power element of training, we will look at what Mager calls "performance discrepancies." Is there a discrepancy between what *should* be done and what *is* being done with things, data, and people? As an example, John has been asked to make a progress report to a committee about a new accounting system being used in the company. John is well qualified because he installed the new system. However, the report was a disaster. Why? John's boss had not trained John on how to make this type of report. Even though John was motivated and had the resources, information, and time, there was performance discrepancy because of his lack of training.

To determine whether or not there is a training problem, the leader should ask:

1. What is the specific task to be accomplished?
2. Does the follower have the specific ability, information, and training to accomplish the task?
3. What are the performance discrepancies between what is being done and what should be done?
4. What are the other possible causes of poor performance other than training? (Motivation, resources, time, environment, and so on).

How to effectively train a follower is another question. The analysis here is to determine if the individual has the specific training to accomplish the task.

Information

The power element of information differs from training. Training results in a change of behavior, the development of a new skill, or gaining new attitudes about something. The information power element concerns procedures and directions of when, where, or who. Time limits, rules to follow, format, specifications, quality requirements, and budget limitations are all examples of information needed to accomplish a task.

The information element requires communication between the leader and the follower. In fact, the follower may have more information about a specific task than does the leader. Communication about information can be negotiated between leader and follower. For example, let's say that Lisa wants Ted to make 30 copies of a report immediately. Ted informs Lisa that the copier takes 20 minutes to warm up. Ted, in this instance, had information about the task to be accomplished that his boss did not have. It is up to Lisa to negotiate the task assignment and keep the lines of communication open so that this situation will not affect production again.

Questions to be asked about the information power element should include these:

1. How much information is available about the task to be accomplished?
2. How much information does the leader have and how much does the follower have?
3. Is there understanding between the leader and follower about time limits, specifications, roles, quality, and so on?
4. Will there be wasted time on tasks because of a lack of information?
5. What is the goal of the task assignment?

In the final analysis the leader assigns the task to the follower, and the information available to the follower affects productivity and performance. In fact, the simple lack of information is one of the biggest problems in most organizations.

Resources

Once someone has reached the position of leader, it is assumed that he or she has certain resources to allocate to followers. For the leader, resources may include such things as information, money, equipment, and power. However, in this analysis of the power elements, we are considering the adequacy of resources for a specific task and for a specific follower. For example, let us say that the follower is a secretary who is well motivated and well trained, has adequate information, and is in a stable environment but whose production is zero. The answer may be simple—production is at a standstill because there is no more paper.

Most organizations work with limited resources. Leaders are constantly identifying objectives and allocating resources. The basic question then is, "Will the organizational objectives be enhanced by the use of these resources in this specific task?" In certain situations it may be better to give more resources to a limited number of goals than to do a poor job with many goals.

In analyzing the power element of resources, several questions should be asked:

1. Is the task necessary to meet organizational objectives?
2. Are there adequate specific resources to accomplish the specific task?
3. Does the follower have access to those resources?
4. Can the task be accomplished by the follower with limited resources?
5. Should a "go, no-go" decision be made in relation to resources?

In a sense, the leader uses his or her personal and position power to find resources for the organization or organizational unit. The leader must then use these resources wisely. By asking questions like those above, leaders can use limited resources to help followers be more productive.

Motivation

The question in the analysis of this power element is not how to motivate but rather how well the follower is motivated to do this specific task. Is the follower motivated or unmotivated? This is also not an easy question. Let us say, for example, that Jim has been in the organization for some time. He has been an excellent worker in the past, yet on one particular day, Jack, the owner of the company, finds Jim sitting in a chair in the back room. Is Jim unmotivated?

Our perceptions and values determine our beliefs about one's motivation. For instance, when Jim says, "Boy, this has been a hard day!" does this indicate he is motivated? We don't really know.

In trying to find indicators of motivation, it is difficult to use followers' comments or even to try to identify their attitude. These are not valid for measuring actual motivation. The personality type of an individual many times confuses us about follower motivation. A person who seems very optimistic about work may in actuality be poorly motivated to accomplish a task. On the other hand, a person who is always complaining about tasks may be highly motivated and perform very well.

We, as leaders, are handicapped by our own frames of reference without realizing it. We can only infer the motivation of a follower by the presence of production. Consequently, there are some questions we should ask about follower motivation:

1. With all other power elements at a satisfactory level, is the follower producing?
2. Are there personal incentives (ones meaningful to the follower) present and associated with the successful completion of the task?
3. Does the follower seem to relate to these incentives by increased production?

Again, the purpose of our analysis of power elements is to find out where we are or what our position power is. However, in the case of motivation, it becomes a matter of degree and calls for a very subjective judgment on the part of the leader. Nevertheless, the analysis is a very useful tool in helping leaders think about production or productivity.

Time

Of all the power elements, time seems to be the most common day-to-day problem. Productivity can suffer because of too much time just as it can with not enough time. It is, however, the use of short segments of time which gives us the most information about followers' time needs. The question in this analysis should be, "Is there adequate time for the follower to accomplish this task?" Bob makes what he thinks is a routine assignment for Jill to accomplish. He leaves Jill to do the work, but when he returns nothing has been done. Upon talking to Jill about the problem, Bob finds out that Jill was interrupted continuously and had no time to complete the assignment.

How we perceive time has an effect on the analysis. There are personality types that are very task-oriented and tend toward crisis management. They see some followers as not having enough urgency about the task. This may be more of a leader's perception problem than reality.

In this analysis, we are trying to determine how time affects the leader's present position when assigning a specific task to a follower. The following questions should be asked about the power element of time:

1. In this specific task, what effect does time have on accomplishing the task?
2. Is the task of such a priority that it overrides other considerations?
3. Will the follower have enough time to complete the task without having problems in quality?
4. Does the use of the follower's time move the organization toward its objectives?
5. Is the lack of time a perception problem or an actual situation?

What we are trying to do with this analysis is determine what type of time constraints there are for the follower on this specific task. The constraints range from crisis situations to long-term projects.

POSITION POWER
AND LEADER BEHAVIOR

When the leader takes the time to analyze each power element in the overall position, he can determine what type of leadership style is more effective under a certain set of circumstances. Although Chapter 6 discusses leadership style and leader behavior, we should understand now that the degree of supervision of a task and follower depends on the overall position at the assignment time.

For instance, when the leader assigns a specific task to a follower who is uninformed, untrained, unmotivated, and so on, the leader's direct supervision will be high. On the other hand, when the power elements are positive, the degree of supervision by the leader is low and the leader can allow the follower to "self-pace" the assigned task.

POSITION ANALYSIS

Figure 4-2 gives us an opportunity to gain a view of our overall power position. The position analysis is a tool in which some subjective judgments are necessary. However, many leaders do not take the

FIGURE 4-2.   Position Analysis.

This exercise helps the leadership to determine the style to be used with an individual or group. The leader gains a view of the overall position by completing this analysis. In addition, the leader should find "soft spots" and be able to adjust his or her leadership accordingly.

NAME OF INDIVIDUAL/GROUP
BEING ANALYZED _____

TASK _____

	Environment	Task	Training	Information	Resources	Motivation	Time
	Certainty	Simple	Trained	Well informed	Adequate	Motivated	Adequate
Q 4							
Q 3							
Q 2							
Q 1							
	Uncertainty	Complex	Untrained	Limited	Limited	Unmotivated	Inadequate

Total _____ ÷ 7 = Q _____

To find the overall position index, add the answers and divide by seven. The degree of supervision moves from High (1) to Low (4). Chart the position index on the line below.

Degree of Supervision	High	Above Average	Below Average	Low
→	Q 1	Q 2	Q 3	Q 4
Leadership Styles	Directive	Developing	Co-Producing	Self-Pacing

time to go through any type of analysis. Yet, two distinct benefits are received. The first is that the leader has some perspective of his or her power position; and second, there will be an indication of which leadership style and behavior has the most potential for success.

In using position analysis, the leader is asked to identify the individual or group being analyzed. It is much easier to analyze one follower than a group. The position analysis asks for a description of the specific task to be accomplished. The leader must make sure that tasks are analyzed in very specific terms.

The next step is for the leader to check the box that indicates the position for the specific power element. Q1 means that there is, for example, uncertainty in the environment, the task is complex, and so on. However, Q4 would mean that the specific power element was low in uncertainty and so on.

As a consequence of the seven analyses of power elements, the leader can find an overall position index by dividing the total of the numbers in each of the boxes by seven. For example, let us say that the leader determines that all of the power elements are at the Q1 level, the total of all the elements is seven and by dividing by seven, the position index is found to be Q1. This would mean that the leader would use a high degree of supervision and the directive style of leadership.

SOFT SPOTS

Another key result of position analysis is the identification of "soft spots" in the overall position. For example, if the position analysis indicates strong power elements except in the area of time, the leader has found a soft spot and will need to modify his or her leadership style accordingly. As the analysis indicates areas of weakness in specific power elements, the leader is given an indication of the areas where greatest improvement may be needed. Providing additional training for a competent follower who works without sufficient information to complete a task will not yield great gains in productivity. Additional information, not training, is the key power element.

In addition, position analysis can assist in the selection of followers to handle certain tasks. While the maturity of a subordinate may be important, it is not the only factor in productivity. For example, leadership styles will change simply because of time limitations, and the leader needs to look at many other factors when making assignments. Yet, many leaders or managers never take these factors into consideration.

It is often easier to assign an employee to a task for which he or she already possesses the appropriate power elements than it is to provide that element to another. In other words, using position analysis uncovers soft spots in task assignments and delegation.

THE NEED
FOR VARIABLE LEADERSHIP

Obviously the elements of power vary from one leadership situation to another. For this reason, the best leadership style will change as the circumstances change. The appropriate leadership style can be determined by analyzing a follower in the terms of a specific task. By using position analysis, we can calculate the style that will have the greatest probability of effectiveness under a given set of circumstances. For example, Frank wanted to assign Bill a report to write. Frank analyzed his and Bill's positions and found everything in order except the power element of resources. Frank immediately recognized that unless Bill had some clerical assistance, the report would never be done. Had Frank not done an analysis, unwarranted emotional conflict could have resulted.

Another key factor is the task-specific nature of the analysis. The subordinate's position is reviewed only in terms of the power elements that apply to a specific task. As the subordinate moves to other tasks, it is clear that new sets of power elements (contingencies) apply. This demands a variation or change in the appropriate leadership style. It is possible, in fact very likely, that a follower will be simultaneously in different power positions in relation to different tasks. Leadership style must vary when supervising these differing tasks. This is not a sign of leader confusion; instead, this is an indication of leader sensitivity to the varying needs of subordinates in relation to varying challenges. As Zalenznik says, "While appointments to positions come from above, affirmation of position comes from below."[9] Leader sensitivity will hasten affirmation.

POLITICS AND POSITION POWER

We have taken a systematic and analytical look at several power elements in the leader's power position. It would be foolish, however, to overlook the realities of politics in position power. As N. H. Martin has observed,

> Executives—whether in business, government, education, or the
> church—have power and use it. They maneuver and manipulate in

order to get a job done and, in many cases, to strengthen and enhance their own position. Although they would hate the thought
and deny the allegation, the fact is that they are politicians. "Politics," according to one of the leading authorities in this complex
and fascinating field, "is . . . concerned with relationships of control
or of influence. To phrase the idea differently, politics deals with
human relationships of superordination and subordination, of dominance and submission, of the governors and the governed." In this
sense, everyone who exercises power must be a politician.[10]

Leaders typically try to enhance each of their power elements. How
successful they are may depend on how good a politician they are.
With resources in short supply, the leader must sometimes play
power games in order to get them.

To summarize, a leader's position of power depends on many
factors in the organization. We should analyze those factors in a systematic way so that more effective leadership approaches can be
made. A leader who does not take the time to calculate the environment, task, information, resources, time, and other factors is wasting
a valuable power tool.

The first step in the analysis is to determine what type of
environment is present in the organization. Is that environment natural or is it a reflection of poor leadership? All of the power elements
should be evaluated in light of the nature of the beast. Leadership
decisions and judgments should be consistent with the characteristics of the organization.

The position analysis described in this chapter can be a valuable tool in not only determining the circumstances in the organization but also in helping the leader determine leadership behaviors
that will be effective. This perspective is one that the average leader
does not take the time to develop. There is, however, no substitute
for careful, organized, and measured analysis of the leader's position
power.

NOTES

1. Paul Pigors, *Leadership or Domination* (Boston, Mass.: Houghton Mifflin
   Company, 1935).
2. Fred E. Fiedler, *A Theory of Leadership Effectiveness* (New York, N.Y.:
   McGraw-Hill Book Company, Inc., 1967).
3. Robert R. Blake and Jane Srygley Mouton, "An Overview of the Grid,"
   Training and Development Journal, May 1975, p. 31.
4. Paul Hersey and Kenneth H. Blanchard, *Management of Organizational
   Behavior*, 4th ed. (Englewood Cliffs, N.J.: Prentice-Hall, Inc., 1982), pp.
   152-55.

5. Don E. Beck, "Beyond the Grid and Situationalism: A Living Systems View," *Training and Development Journal*, Aug. 1982, p. 79.
6. Hersey and Blanchard, *Management of Organizational Behavior*, p. 152. See model, Figure 7-1.
7. Amitai Etzioni, *Modern Organizations* (Englewood Cliffs, N.J.: Prentice-Hall, 1964), p. 61.
8. Robert I. Mager, *Analyzing Performance Problems* (Belmont, Calif.: Fearon Pitman Publishing, Inc., 1970), p. 1.
9. Abraham Zaleznik, "Power and Politics in Organizational Life," *Readings in Managerial Psychology*, 2nd ed., ed. Harold J. Leavitt (Chicago, Ill.: University of Chicago Press, 1973), p. 303.
10. N. H. Martin and J. H. Sims, "Power Tactics," *Readings in Managerial Psychology*, 2nd ed., ed. Harold J. Leavitt (Chicago, Ill.: University of Chicago Press, 1973), p. 272.

5

Personal Power

Turning a *minus* into a *plus* is a part of our human nature. How we do it is called our "style of life," or personality. Overcoming weakness can be a creative force in our life and can result in greater personal power. In addition, knowing our personality and how it affects others can help us gain personal power. For instance, Bill is the new owner of a company which has lost money for the past several years. Obviously Bill is operating from a position of weakness and must turn things around. Because he needs a great deal of help from his staff, Bill must enlist their support for some needed changes. The influence he develops with the members of his staff will be determined to a large extent by his personality.

The ability we have to influence others—apart from our organization, office, or position—is our personal power. The skills we have developed, our knowledge, our expertise, and our ability to get along with others are all examples of personal power. We bring personal power to the situation; consequently, it is not something given to us by someone else. Ike, our World War II general, demonstrated his ability to overcome a larger and better-equipped invading force. Because he turned a minus into a plus, he was chosen by the American people to be President. Ike was able not only to deal with a crisis situation but with the people in those circumstances. He developed what people perceived as a strong personal appeal.

LEADERSHIP TRAITS

Some people seem to be better at overcoming weaknesses than others. Throughout history we have picked them out and made leaders of them. What made them leaders? As James Owens has said, "Trait theorists contended early in this century that there was a finite set of personal characteristics, inner traits, which distinguished effective from ineffective leaders."[1] The idea was that if we could identify specific leadership traits, we could then train all leaders to be effective. One of the most successful field generals during World War II was General George Patton. However, the personality traits that served him well in combat situations were totally inappropriate for the diplomatic tasks required of an Allied commander. The same traits that brought him honor in the battlefield almost destroyed his career when the shooting was far away.

Unfortunately, no set of common leadership traits useful in all situations was found. Again Owens points out:

> From the beginning of leadership research in this century, even early trait theorists had noted as an obstacle traits required in a leader seem to depend, to some extent, on the demands of the particular situation and specific classes of followers. The factor of situation, the particular environment in which the leader happened to be, had been purposely eliminated from the research designs of both the trait and behavior theorists. The ideal they sought was a leader profile (a set of traits or behaviors), universally valid as a predictor or descriptor of what a leader is, independently of changing circumstances or followers or situations; just as qualities such as human courage, self-confidence, physical strengths or communication skill operate and continue to be useful in all situations.[2]

If no set of universally valid personality traits in leaders can be found, then what part does personality play in leadership? We all know individuals who are well-educated but who lack the qualities of leadership. On the other hand, some less-educated individuals seem to be "natural" leaders. We also know individuals of seemingly equal talent, education, and ability; one has a leadership personality, and the other one does not. Certainly the personality dimension is too important to be overlooked.

PERSONALITY:
A FRAME OF REFERENCE

Alfred Adler concluded that by the age of five, a child has formed character traits, or a "style of life," which is more or less permanently fixed.[3] The human being, it seems, inherently requires a frame of reference in order to function as a person. The personality of an individual serves as that frame of reference. While, for instance, some people seem to be competing all of the time, other individuals are satisfied to be team members. Still others like to be around people, telling stories and talking. People become systematic in the way they act and tend to be predictable in their behavior.

Personality reveals itself in all the activities and attitudes of the human being. Personality traits are projected into every situation, and this is how we achieve our uniqueness through what may be called our "style of life." Yet that uniqueness finds expression only in relation to the organization or community of other human beings. This can be seen in groups as small as the family unit. Each child is different and is continuously finding ways to express those differences with parents and other members of the family.

With personality relatively fixed over our lifetime and serving as our frame of reference, the study of basic personality traits can give us the ability to understand and predict our followers' behaviors. If we know that Mary's personality type allows her to work well with people but that she has a hard time with procedural matters, we can avoid many problems. This is why we cannot abandon personality research in leadership.

PERCEPTION

In human beings, feelings of strengths and weaknesses are based on self-comparison of ourselves with other members of a group. The result of this self-comparison is our own self-perception or self-concept. The self-concept gives us, as Adler suggested, a frame of reference—no matter that it is not entirely accurate. For instance, if we think we are good at sports, it helps give us a frame of reference. Yet the perception of how good or how poor we are in sports will not be the same as the reality. However, our perception of ourselves gives meaning to our life and a way for each of us to function psychologically.

As a practical matter, how we perceive ourselves and others has a profound effect on our leadership. The most effective leaders are able to adjust to the changing situation, and they perceive themselves as finding a common frame of reference in all circumstances. When dealing with others, effective leaders also find ways of communicating with different types of personalities. Some leaders, for example, seem to have a knack for treating followers a special way depending on their individual personality. Somehow the effective leader finds the key to the productive behavior of the follower.

CHANGING PERCEPTIONS

If, as Adler believed, personality is relatively stable throughout life, what makes us go through so many emotional highs and lows? When we move from a position of strength to a position of weakness in a given situation, there is an emotional reaction. For instance, if we lose a job or a loved one, we feel a loss of strength of power. Our power base has been diminished, and compared to before we are in an inferior emotional position. Because our equilibrium is upset, our emotional state is threatened.[4]

As far as perception is concerned, it is not so much our personality (style of life) or self-concept which changes as it is our personal power base. The gain or loss of individual power changes our behavior more than it changes our basic personality. We would feel good in a swimming group where we could perform and be competitive. Our power base would not be threatened. However, we would feel a loss of power in a tennis group where everyone played better than we did. It is not likely that either situation would affect our basic personality or self-concept.

Again, the average individual's personality tends to be relatively constant throughout life. It is our power-base shifts that change our behavior.

Factors changing throughout life are shown in Figure 5-1.

FIGURE 5-1. Changing Factors.

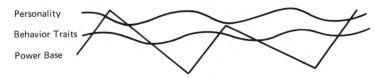

As we can see, how we deal with our ever-changing personal power base becomes very important. In each new situation, the leader must recognize how to overcome weaknesses and help followers to do the same. To turn a minus into a plus is not only good practice but is one of humanity's basic psychological drives. It can be as simple as a child's learning to ride a bike or as complicated as a businessperson's turning around an ailing company. The human being's basic desire is for achievement and to be recognized for that achievement.

PERSONALITY TYPES

If, then, the style of life is more or less stable, can we identify what type of personality an individual has? If we could, leaders would have a basis by which to understand and on which to predict and plan for certain types of behavior from followers. Furthermore, the leader's personal power would increase and organizational goals would be more likely to be accomplished. As an example, suppose Mary had an assignment she needed accomplished. By knowing Bob's personality type, she could predict his reaction, anticipate the kinds of questions he would ask, and plan an effective leadership approach with him. Her personal power would increase with Bob because he feels more comfortable with Mary and the assignment.

Recent research indicates that there are indeed specific personality types which can be measured. Two major research tracks are beginning to show that personality is determined by (1) dominant styles of behavior as an individual's frame of reference and (2) brain-hemisphere-controlled behavior clusters. For example, if we are good at bookkeeping or accounting, it is because of our personality type, and our type may be a function of the brain hemisphere that is dominant or controls our behavior.

Two kinds of instruments have been developed which show four distinct styles of dominant personality traits. The Brain Domination Instrument by Ned Herrmann[5] and the many instruments developed from William M. Marston's[6] work in 1928 all show and measure the dominant styles of behavior in individuals. Although the two research tracks have taken different approaches, the similarity of the results is striking. Figure 5-2 indicates the personality types found as a result of each study.

As a result of adapting and expanding Marston's and Herrmann's works, the authors of this book have developed a basic description of each of the four types of personality, sometimes referred to as B.E.S.T.

Bold (B)

The Bold personality is stimulated by the challenge of a new adventure. There is a need for dominance over the situation and other people. The Bold style is good when quick decisions and results are needed. However, long-range planning and direction may be a problem.

PERSONALITY STYLES

	1	2	3	4
William Marston	Dominance adventurous competitive direct inventive bold pioneer	Inducement affectionate expressive fluent inspiring optimistic talkative	Submission accomodating considerate generous loyal moderate sympathetic	Compliance calculating cautious exacting logical precise strict
Ned Herrmann	Creative synthesizer visual conceptual	Interpersonal emotional talker expressive	Controlled conservative organization procedural	Logical analyzer technical quantita- tive

FIGURE 5-2.   Personality Style Research Tracks.

The Bold-style individual likes straightforward communications, which may give the impression of bluntness. The High B is independent and likes to work alone. However, this creates problems because of failure to delegate or to get help with major projects.

The Bold-style individual needs to be sensitive to the needs of people. Otherwise, in rushing to get the job done, the High B may tend toward crisis management. Long-range planning, relaxing around others, and softer communciations will help the Bold personality become more effective.

Marston used such terms as *aggressiveness, initiative, determination, power, strength of character*, and *bulldog-like qualities* to describe the Bold personality style. Herrmann saw him as an *entrepreneur, conceptualizer, synthesizer* and a *daydreamer*. The Bold-style personality, then, is one who likes getting quick results, accepts challenges, makes quick decisions, expedites action, makes bold changes, and is a problem solver. General George Patton, for example, was a Bold-type personality. At one time in his career, he was afraid the war would pass him by. There was no question of his need to be dominant over his troops and of his straightforward manner of speaking.

Expressive (E)

The Expressive personality is stimulated by being around others and persuading them to his or her point of view. There is a need to be an influence over others. The High E is good with people and generates a positive and enthusiastic environment. However, working or being alone may become a problem.

The Expressive-style individual likes to talk and is generally good at it. Outgoing, neighborly, optimistic, and confident, the High E may have a problem with time conrol and objectivity.

Expressive-style individuals need to be aware of their impact on other people. They need to control details and to work more with specific objectives in mind. Because of their feelings for people, High E's may tend to delegate too much. At times being overly optimistic can be a problem.

For the Expressive-personality type, Marston used terms like *persuasive, convincing, luring, charming, appealing, selling, inducing,* and *winning.* Herrmann's description of this type individual would include terms like *interpersonal, emotional, talker,* and *expressive.* The Expressive-style personality, consequently, likes contact with people, is enthusiastic, speaks well, can motivate others, and exhibits poise in front of groups. Ronald Reagan, like many politicians, can be classified as a High E. Reagan is good with words, is perceived as warm and friendly, and is most often optimistic.

Sympathetic (S)

The Sympathetic personality is most often patient, dependable, loyal, and a good listener. The High S individual needs to belong and to serve. High S's are hard workers, productive, and willing to be followers. However, working for work's sake and feeling secure in that work may be a problem.

The High S likes security and the status quo and will generally give long service, be persistent, even-tempered, and amicable. However procrastination and a lack of urgency may be a problem at times.

The Sympathetic-style individual needs to learn to adjust quickly to unexpected changes and to be more assertive when necessary. Because of the need for security, the High S may be too possessive with information, space, and things.

Marston's terms for the Sympathetic-type individual would include *willing, good-natured, tender-hearted, obliging, accommodating,* and *unselfish.* Herrmann's corresponding type would be described as *conservative, procedural, sequential, controlled,* and *administrative.* The High S style is one in which the individual performs to standards, exhibits patience, is loyal, and develops specialized skills. Because of the personality, this person would be a long-term employee, a hard worker, and a good listener. An example is Joe who has been with the company for 20 years. Joe likes his job and works after hours when needed. He never says anything bad about the organization or the boss. Joe is almost like the natural follower except when he is confronted by an aggressive person. Sometimes that makes him slow down or withdraw.

Technical (T)

The Technical personality is one who is controlled, cautious, precise, and rule-oriented. There is a need for a sense of order. The High T-style individual has an orientation toward planning and accuracy. At times, he or she may be called a perfectionist.

High T's like to be thorough and are serious about quality standards. They try to reduce risks through logical thinking, are persuaded by facts, and are willing to listen to details. However, a lack of self-confidence may be a problem.

The Technical-style individual needs to develop self-confidence and a tolerance for confusion and conflict. Also, the ability to make quicker decisions as necessary would help. Because of the tendency toward rules, the High T should be able to use a more flexible style when needed.

Marston's own terms for the Technical type would include *cautious, conforming, disciplined, realistic, yielding to standards*, and *respect*. The authors have modified Marston's concept of this personality type because it was felt that this type was more orderly and controlling. It is felt that the term "technical" better describes this type of personality and gives more contrast between Marston's submissive personality types. Herrmann's concept of this personality type comes closer and supports the authors' construct. Herrmann's more vivid description of the Technical type includes *logical, analyzer, technical, rational, quantitative*, and *cognitive*. Consequently, the Technical-style personality follows directions, concentrates on details, and controls quality. A good example of a High T was Jimmy Carter. He once said of his Presidency that he presented engineer-like solutions to national problems. He identified the problem, gave possible solutions, and then proposed an answer.

WHY DIFFERENT PERSONALITY TYPES?

The study of personality not only has psychological significance but also involves the fields of philosophy and religion. Personality is at the very heart of what it means to be human. Just as human beings receive meaning from their personalities, each individual human being receives meaning from his or her style of life. We are bound by what Adler called the "Law of Movement" in which each of us moves to a different tempo, rhythm, and direction. Thus, we are all different. While Bob likes to travel, Bill would rather stay at home. In contrast to Sandra who likes a lively argument, Patricia likes quiet conversation. We respond to the same situation each in our own way.

Although William M. Marston recognized that normal emotional responses came from the central nervous system, his division of the personality into four types was based on emotions which he perceived to be alliance vs. antagonism or superior vs. inferior relationships. In other words, Marston's four personality types were expressions of the normal emotions of dominance, inducement, submission, and compliance.

Many other researchers have concluded that our personality type is a function of which brain hemisphere dominates our actions. In fact, Ned Herrmann believes that there are four, not two, types of brain specialization. Most human beings become dominant in one or more of these brain specializations. The four learning types, according to Herrmann, are "open-minded," "feelings," "controlled," and "facts."

It must be pointed out that human beings have different mixtures of the four personality types. Some individuals do not even show a dominant style on a personality profile instrument. However, most of us have one personality type that guides our behavior. Some individuals are very dominant in one style, and this is very evident in their behavior.

It is not the purpose of the study of the four personality types to force an individual into a negative category. In fact, each personality type has its strengths and weaknesses. It is only by knowing these strengths and weaknesses that we overcome nonproductive behavior as leaders.

The purpose of this review was to point out that personality is more than an environmental accident. We now know that there are personality types and that these types can be measured. As a result, the leader has much more information about people upon which to make task assignments, production decisions, and judgments about people. For example, the leader can predict that the Expressive personality (High E) will most likely work well with others and can even be used to sell ideas or products. Moreover, the High T can help control the quality of ideas and products. In addition, the leader, by studying personality types, can know the weaknesses of each and can adjust the task assignments to fit them.

INTERACTION OF PERSONALITY TYPES

Each personality type responds to the same situation in a different way. If everyone in the organization needed to learn to operate a new type of equipment, the possible reactions would range from enthusiasm to caution to a feeling of challenge to resentment.

The wants and needs of the different types are not the same. However, individuals of all personality types must work and live together. If a leader can anticipate the interaction of the personality types, more productive use of followers can be made, and at the same time many personality conflict problems can be avoided. Figure 5-3 describes the wants and needs of each of the personalities previously discussed. Notice the possibilities for teamwork and also the potential for conflict.

FIGURE 5-3.   Wants and Needs of Personalities.

Most people are not aware of their dominant behavior style and how it shapes their reaction to other individuals. For example, when asked about his first meeting with Ronald Reagan after Reagan's election, Jimmy Carter said he was very disappointed. Former President Carter indicated that he had a list of 20 items arranged in priority order to talk about with Reagan. He further explained that President-elect Reagan did not seem interested because he did not even take notes.

It is obvious in this observation by Carter that he is a High T (Technical). List-making and note-taking are good indications of T personalities. President Reagan is most likely a High E (Expressive) because of his communications ability. High E's are not prone to take notes.

Because of the interaction of the four personality types, the leader should

1. understand each type of personality,
2. anticipate how each will react to a task assignment,
3. help build understanding of the four personality types with each member of the team or organization,
4. make assignments based on the follower's personality strengths, and
5. understand his or her own personality.

PERSONALITY AND LEADERSHIP

Emotional conflict is a problem in all organizations. How much of a problem it becomes is to a large extent the responsibility of the leader. As Zaleznik has said, "Because power problems are the effects of personality on structure, the solutions demand thinking which is free from the disabilities of emotional conflicts."[7] Emotional conflicts happen because we have little understanding of our own personality or how it reacts to other personality types. For instance, if Alex was the owner of a department store and was a High B, he could cause a great deal of stress and conflict without being aware of it. Alex may think everyone is operating the same way he does. That is, he may think that everyone likes constant change, quick results, and the challenges of the business world. Alex, by not understanding other personality types, will create much emotional conflict and stress in his department store.

The leader can reduce organizational conflict and increase productivity by

1. helping subordinates understand their own personality types,

2. showing subordinates how other personality types behave,

3. teaming personality types according to the task to be accomplished,

4. teaching followers how to communicate with the different personality types, and

5. using personality analysis as one factor in evaluating organization performance.

When leaders take the time to demonstrate this kind of concern for followers, the personal power of the leader is increased.

Leaders have personalities, too. The expectation of how an organization is to be led may be more a function of the leader's personality than any other factor. For instance, a leader with a High B personality will want quick results, make frequent changes, and may make the majority of organizational decisions. On the other hand, a leader with a High T personality may require many procedural rules, expect high-quality work from employees, and take a long time to make changes.

If only we could define the common elements of leadership, then supposedly the successful leader could incorporate those traits into his or her own life. Like the Scout who is supposed to be loyal, brave, reverent, clean, and courteous, the leader could take on those characteristics of effective leadership and achieve greater results. Unfortunately, even if a list of effective traits was developed and commonly agreed upon as important to leadership success, little value would be produced by this effort. Regardless of a person's dedication to a cause, basic personality will make him or her unique and unable to perfectly mimic the prescribed leadership traits. For instance, even the most dedicated Scout fails to be perfectly loyal, thrifty, reverent, clean, and courteous.

How do leaders increase their personal power in the organization? The real strength of a leader comes from followers, not the organizational position held. Inevitably, over the long run, it is the follower who gives the leader the power to lead. Richard Nixon found this out. He was elected by a landslide vote but after a few months was relieved of his power. In the United States, there is a great expectation of elected officials, and the people react to the abuse of power.

Because personality affects personal power, leaders should

1. be aware of their basic personality,

2. be aware of how personality affects the performance and actions of others,

3. learn how their own personality influences followers, and

4. be aware of how personality is affected by circumstances.

The reduction of personality conflicts in an organization increases the likelihood that each individual's personal power will grow. While organizational positions are limited and scarce, there is no such scarcity for personal power. Consequently, each individual in an organization from the bottom to the top can make a more productive contribution. The understanding of personality and personality types facilitates the growth of personal power. Again, this is the leader's responsibility.

OTHER TYPES OF PERSONAL POWER

Amitai Etzioni defined personal power as the extent to which followers respect, are committed to, and feel good about their leader and see their goals as being satisfied by the goals of their leader.[8] These "powers" are qualities that are within individuals as they move from situation to situation. It is, however, the projection of these qualities that influences followers.

The concept of personal power is relatively general in nature. There are an infinite number of types or combinations of personal power subgroups. Any type of leader influence or power which develops in the follower a willingness to be led is personal power. Theorists have identified the following types of personal power:

Expert Power

The leader who exhibits expert power has inherently or has developed special expertise, skill, or understanding in a specific area. Followers see this leader as a source who is able to solve problems and facilitate production. For instance, an airplane pilot is an expert. During the course of a flight, the pilot adjusts the plane's speed, path, and altitude in order to have a successful trip. The passengers trust the pilot to have the expertise and skill to provide safe transportation.[9]

Referent Power

When referent power exists, followers admire the leader's personality. There is an identification with the leader based on admiration. Many times children relate to TV or movie characters. The identification is so strong that children try to emulate their heros. Moreover, adults tend to place tremendous emphasis on their leader's personality. We are influenced by leaders with positive personality characteristics.[10]

Persuasive Power

The persuasive leader is able to convince followers to comply, regardless of the factual evidence. In other words, followers are influenced by the good talker, even if they know the leader is wrong. When a leader is enthusiastic and optimistic and is able to motivate followers because they want to believe, the leader is exercising persuasive power over followers. For example, the boss who persuades employees that business is getting better, even though customer traffic is down, is using persuasive power.

Association Power

This leader is perceived as having power because of his or her friendship or companionship with other powerful people. They key word is "perceived." There is a perception of power assigned to the leader; and in many instances, the leader is unaware of the impact of association power. A good example of association power is described by John Ehrlichman, former Presidential counsel, about his relationship with Richard Nixon:

> At first I didn't understand how much power I derived from simply being the President's counsel, with an office in the West Wing of the White House and being written about as a member of the President's senior staff.
>
> Within 60 days I was in Europe laying out the President's trip to eight countries, dealing with ambassadors, foreign officials and our military. I discovered that these people considered my word to be law! I spoke for the President, and in our government that made me King of the Mountain.
>
> I realized that my power was wholly derivative; apart from the President I was nothing. But with his explicit or implicit backing, I could (and did) hire, fire and order about such disparate agencies as the Corps of Engineers, the Bureau of Roads, the Bureau of Indian Affairs and the Federal Reserve Board.
>
> The perquisites which attach to Presidential power are both delightful and seductive.[11]

Comparison Power

This power is rather negative but still valid. In this instance, a leader emerges through the process of elimination. When this type of personal power is achieved, it is because other possible leaders were not selected and the individual is the only possibility left. It is when a leader emerges out of a team or group because no one else seems to have any leadership talent. For example, Bob, Bill, and Mary are compared by followers and Mary selected. That is, Bob and Bill were eliminated rather than Mary's having actually been selected.

SUMMARY

It is amazing that the major programs on leadership so effectively marketed today ignore the basic and primary element of personality style. We first respond to another individual based on that individual's personality and how well it relates to our own. Our perception of the other person gives order to our social environment. Over the years we learn to identify strong and weak personality traits in other people. This is a subtly but extremely important process. Early in our relationship with another person questions of power, ambition, credibility, confidence, dependability, and rationality are tentatively answered. We incorporate this perception into our relationship with the other person. This is a process that cannot be divorced from our social or professional life.

Perhaps leadership theorists have ignored the issue of personality because it has been hard to appropriately define. Characteristics, styles, manners, traits, attitudes, and so on all mix together to form our way of describing another's personality. Since such factors have not been easy to quantify, they have not been appropriate for those who build models and wish to cloak their products with the appearance of being scientific and qualifiably proven.

Research is now beginning to tell us that personality style is based on measurable reasons and not just on environmental accidents. Personality may be defined in terms of dominant behavior patterns. These patterns may be brain-hemisphere controlled or otherwise controlled by some biosociologic factor.

In addition, leaders must understand other subgroups of personal powers at work in the organization. Expert, referent, persuasive, association, and comparison are but a few of the many types of personal powers. Gaining personal power comes from

1. understanding personality types,
2. using the strengths of each type personality,
3. increasing personal expertise through training and reading,
4. making every effort to communicate to followers a sense of caring and concern with increased human relations activities,
5. communicating with followers with personality type in mind, and recognizing the followers' own personal power when they turn a minus into a plus.

In conclusion, the beginning of the acquisition of personal power comes with self-knowledge. The use of personal power is a struggle for significance, recognition, and achievement for the leader as well as for the follower.

NOTES

1. James Owens, "A Reappraisal of Leadership Theory and Training," *Personnel Administrator*, Nov. 1981, p. 76.
2. Ibid. p. 80
3. Ira Progoff, *The Death and Rebirth of Psychology*, (New York, N.Y.: McGraw-Hill Book Company, 1973), p. 59.
4. Ibid. p. 56.
5. Elizabeth S. Gorovitz, "The Creative Brain II: A Revisit with Ned Herrmann," *Training and Development Journal*, Dec. 1982, pp. 74-88.
6. William M. Marston, *Emotions of Normal People* (Minneapolis, Minn.: Persona Press, Inc., 1979).
7. Abraham Zaleznik, "Power and Politics in Organizational Life," *Readings in Managerial Psychology*, 2nd ed., ed. Harold J. Leavitt (Chicago, Ill.: University of Chicago Press, 1973), p. 304.
8. Amitai Etzioni, *A Comparative Analysis of Complex Organizations* (New York, N.Y.: The Free Press, 1961).
9. J. R. P. French and B. Raven, "The Bases of Social Power," in D. Cartwright, *Studies in Social Power* (Ann Arbor, Mich.: University of Michigan, Institute for Social Research, 1959).
10. Ibid.
11. John Ehrlichman, "What I Have Learned," *Parade Magazine*, Sept. 26, 1982, pp. 4-5.

6

Action Power

We have all heard guest speakers talk about effective leadership. They generally use terms such as *motivated, democratic, initiative, responsible, enthusiastic,* and so on. Many speakers go to great lengths to describe the leadership behaviors or styles that promote success. While most of these behaviors sound good, they represent only generalizations.

The study of leadership behaviors or styles, however, is somewhat of a fallback position. Since personality trait research and contingency theories tended to confuse the definition of effective leadership, theorists began to look for specific behaviors that leaders could use to increase productivity. Unfortunately, the early behavior theorists found no consistent behavior or style appropriate to all situations. Once again research had failed to prove how effective leaders should behave in all leadership circumstances.

However, researchers continued to identify leadership behaviors and to classify them. Terms like "democratic," "autocratic," "laissez-faire," "bureaucratic," and "consultative leadership" became popular. Leaders were identified by these sterotypes, and reputations were built (or lost) because of them. For instance, educational administration students were told that the democratic leadership style was the only appropriate style to use in the school setting.

Leaders began to deliberately behave in ways that reflected one style of behavior. Consequently, leaders tended to study and develop specific styles that they thought were most effective for them. Leaders selected role models whom they felt filled the selected sterotype. Specific methodologies were then developed to use with each type of leadership. As far as the democratic style was concerned, for instance, the leader was told to hold meetings, ask followers for their opinions about tasks, and have a suggestion box. In time, however, other methods were developed to help leaders "say no" and to use "hard-nose management."

Another problem with the development of a specific style by a leader was that many times personality got in the way. The leader was told that one style was best for a given situation, but the leader's personality conflicted with that style. What developed was the need to understand how leadership styles could be used effectively and how personality influenced the process.

POSITION AND LEADERSHIP STYLE

In Chapter 4, we discussed the leader's position and position power. It was determined that different leadership styles depended on the overall power position of the leader and follower. In this chapter, we will discuss what specific types of leadership actions we should use in a given set of circumstances.

Again in Chapter 4, we identified four types of leadership behaviors—directing, developing, coproducing, and self-pacing. These behaviors were selected because they correspond to the human "power cycle." That is, in every situation we perceive ourselves as being somewhere along a power continuum or power cycle. We may, for instance, think we can accomplish a task without any help; we feel independent. On the other hand, we may feel the need of a great deal of help on some other task. Our perception of our power cycle level is different on each task.

Human beings continually compare themselves to others. They may feel superior or inferior based on that comparison. Their power base is a perception of where they are along the power cycle at any given moment. For instance, in one situation we may feel inferior and need help learning the basics of the task, somewhat like learning how to play tennis. However, as we progress up the power cycle and through the power cycle process, we begin to feel more successful. In fact, we may feel superior to others who are just starting their tennis lessons.

The power cycle is characterized by several steps or levels. The individual moves from level one where the basics of a task are learned to level two where more development takes place. In level two, we learn to communicate, ask intelligent questions, and interact as a team member with others. Level three begins when we are able to make a contribution to the decision-making process, test our ideas with others, and share some responsibility. At level four we can accept the responsibility for our own actions as well as for the actions of others. Our leadership of others takes place in level four. We have learned the task and can now direct others in their power cycle task development. Let us say, for example, that Mike is a janitor in a large building. Tim, his boss, asks him to wax the halls, even though Mike is not familiar with the procedure. Tim must spend time showing Mike how to wax, and as soon as Mike has mastered the basics, Tim should expand his explanation of the procedure. For instance, Tim will need to tell Mike that by doing one side of the hall at a time, others will not be inconvenienced.

Tim now recognizes that Mike understands the procedure and, in fact, can make improved procedural decisions that Tim had not considered. Tim learns to trust Mike and feels that Mike is now ready to accept full responsibility for the task. Mike is motivated to do a good job because of Tim's trust.

The power cycle can take only a few moments, or it can take a great amount of time. It depends on the task assignment. The leader must recognize the follower's power cycle level for a given task and start from there.

Figure 6-1 helps us understand how the power cycle works. Notice that movement can be both ways and that in order to reach level four, we must progress through each of the other levels. The power cycle depicts the movement of an individual's power base in acquiring the skills and understanding for a new task. Moreover, the power cycle may be useful in viewing the life process of humans.

The power cycle is very much like life. We are told what to do and given much direction as infants. This first power cycle level is where we learn the basic powers of how, what, and when to do. Depending on the individual, this period lasts until about five years of age. The second level of the power cycle is reached when the child learns how to behave around and team with others. Many social and interpersonal communications skills are developed during this phase. This period most often lasts during the period of the individual's schooling. The third level in the cycle is the point at which the individual starts making a contribution to the solution of problems in the organization or society. This could include work, research, church, politics, and so on but most often involves working with others. The individual begins to share decision-making responsibilities with others. The final level occurs when the individual is able to take full responsibility for his or her own behavior in socially

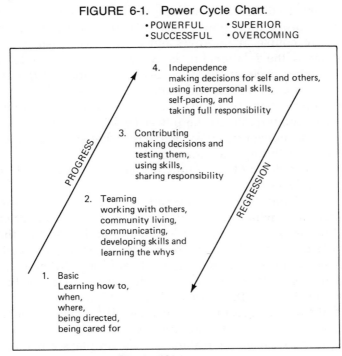

FIGURE 6-1. Power Cycle Chart.

•POWERFUL   •SUPERIOR
•SUCCESSFUL •OVERCOMING

4. Independence
   making decisions for self and others,
   using interpersonal skills,
   self-pacing, and
   taking full responsibility

3. Contributing
   making decisions and
   testing them,
   using skills,
   sharing responsibility

PROGRESS

REGRESSION

2. Teaming
   working with others,
   community living,
   communicating,
   developing skills and
   learning the whys

1. Basic
   Learning how to,
   when,
   where,
   being directed,
   being cared for

•INFERIOR   •UNSUCCESSFUL
•OVERCOME   •POWERLESS

acceptable ways. An individual in this fourth level has "earned the right" to lead and direct others and possesses the skills because of the progress through the power cycle. The life power cycle moves from an inferior to a superior position.

How does the leader facilitate the power cycle process for followers? What styles of leadership work best for each level of the cycle? Is the leader in a helping relationship with followers? Again, the power cycle concept and model gives us a view of the follower's status on a given task. Each task will be different, even within the same individual. This simple model can help us to avoid asking a follower to perform a task he or she is not ready for or to take on more responsibility. It all depends on the specific task and the power cycle status of the follower.

POWER AND LEADERSHIP STYLES

As Alfred Adler once observed, man is driven from within himself, as by a blind teleology, ever striving toward goals he cannot see, seeking to overcome his inferiority by reaching toward perfection.[1]

We as leaders need to facilitate this growth in followers. We should help them improve their power base or ability to handle new tasks. Ultimately, of course, it improves our own power base.

What is the relationship between the leader's style and the follower's power cycle status? The leader can analyze the status of the follower on a given task and then facilitate the follower's growth from that point. Many times the follower will tell the leader where he feels most comfortable on the power cycle. The follower will give both verbal and nonverbal cues about his or her status without being aware of such a thing as a power cycle.

Here is a description of how leaders help followers in each of the power cycle levels.

In level one (Basics) leadership is a process of helping followers learn how, when, where, and so on and to become oriented to the situation or task. The style of leadership is that of directing. It is the leader's responsibility to more closely supervise the activity of the follower because the power elements are low. Ultimately, the directing behavior in level one saves the leader time later in the cycle. Followers must know the basics before tasks can be accomplished and the follower can accept more responsibility. One common problem among leaders is that they assume that followers can already perform a task. Because, for instance, a person plays a piano, it does not mean that he or she can write music. Even level of education is not always an indication of performance ability. The leader must always be on guard not to assume too much about the follower's skills. Spot checks of the follower's understanding and skill on a given task should be made.

In level two (Teaming) there is a process of helping followers understand why a task should be done a specific way. In addition, learning how the task relates to the overall organization and to others in the organization is emphasized. Followers need to learn to work with others; being a member of the team becomes important at this point. Consequently, communication is an important part of the learning process for the follower. Only when followers learn these skills can they move on to the next level. The leader's responsibility is to help followers develop these skills. The leader uses the developing style of leadership at this point in the power cycle.

Every task has a purpose and relates to other tasks being done by others in the organization. In level two, the follower learns many teaming and interpersonal skills necessary to gain cooperation from others. It is, consequently, not only the task skills that are important but also the human relationship skills that develop in level two.

Level three (Contributing) denotes the time when the follower is ready to make contributions to the decision-making process in an intelligent and informed manner. In a sense, the follower has earned this role because of moving up to level three. It is the leader's responsibility at this point to help the follower make decisions and to test those decisions. The leader must make the follower feel that careful decision-making and participation will be rewarded. Consequently, the leader's style in level four should be coproducing in nature. The leader and follower discuss problems, procedures, and solutions and arrive at a joint decision. Let us say, for example, that Jane has been in sales for some time. She has experience and has performed well. Because of her success in selling, her boss asks her to evaluate a new product. They discuss the pros and cons in an open and frank manner. Improvements are made in the product because of Jane's input, and Jane feels that she has made a real contribution to the company.

At level four (Independence) the follower is ready to assume full responsibility for the accomplishment of the task. The follower has proven to be worthy of trust because of past performance and can self-direct task activities. The leadership style is one of delegating or helping followers self-pace their own activities. Again, trust is the key word, and in the power cycle the follower is able to become more independent. If we were to follow Jane as she moves into level four, we may find that her boss would give her a new product to evaluate. Jane would take the new product to her office, study it, and make her recommendations to her boss about changes. Jane makes independent and responsible judgments, and her boss has trust in her.

From the standpoint of the leader, the four styles of leadership behavior we find useful in the power cycle are Directing, level 1; Developing, level 2; Coproducing, level 3; and Self-pacing, level 4. The power cycle levels for the follower are, from one to four; Basics, Teaming, Contributing, and Independence. The follower moves from a power position of inferiority to superiority with specific tasks, and the leader facilitates that movement. Again we can see the relationship between the Power Management Model and the follower's Power Cycle Model. If the leader is interested in a strong organization, he or she will assist followers up the power cycle. These models offer some concrete methods of doing just that.

PROBLEMS IN THE POWER CYCLE

As Adler pointed out, the organism that does not overcome its inferiority falls by the wayside. This is true for organizations as well as individuals. We see it every day. Leaders who find themselves in trouble because of their personality, position, or leadership behavior will fall by the wayside. One of the most often overlooked facts of power is that it is given by the consent of the governed. The more positive power the individual follower has, the more power the leader has. While it is easy for us to see this in government, it is no less true in business and education. The leader who uses intimidation, fear, coercion, and yelling as part of his or her leadership style will not last long as a leader. Workers in our society will no longer tolerate this type of behavior.

There is a kind of accountability for today's leaders. We see this most dramatically when high-performance technical employees are promoted to a supervisory position. When the new supervisory role is changed to include the human relations factor, many problems arise. The employee is no longer repsonsible for his own work but the work of others. How effective the supervisor's leadership is will be reflected in productivity.

One plant manager explained that when problems come up in production, the supervisor and worker go behind the building and fight it out. Even though it is hard for us to imagine this happening, some have the mistaken idea that it is helpful. The fact that the plant had a high turnover, a strong and active union, and low production did not seem to matter.

Problems arise in the power cycle for two reasons: the leader uses the wrong leadership style with the follower, or the follower perceives he or she is in another level other than the one the leader is using. These power cycle problems are called "negative power discrepancies." The relationship and interaction between leader and follower are negative.

For instance, there would be a negative power discrepancy if the leader treated the follower using level four leadership style when the follower felt he or she should be in level one. The leader's perception is out of phase with what the follower can actually do. For this specific task, the stage is set for failure and all the emotional conflicts associated with it.

The interaction between the leader and follower does not need to be a negative relationship. Leaders must lead and followers must follow or leadership is not taking place. Again, this does not mean there must be an adversary relationship between the two. Negative power discrepancy can be caused by the leader or the follower. Discrepancies occur because

1. the leader did not use the most productive leadership behavior,
2. the leader did not analyze the follower's power position,
3. the leader was not aware of how personality affects the interaction,

4. the follower had the wrong expectation about the task, and (or)
5. the follower had the wrong expectations about the leader/subordinate relationship.

When the leader/follower relationship is positive, both parties have a comfortable overall relationship. The leader is able to influence the follower to contribute to the accomplishment of the organizational goals. This means that there is no negative power discrepancy and that the relationship is based on positive power. Let's say that Bob needs Liz to prepare a report for a committee meeting. Bob understands Liz has never done this type of report before. He realizes that his leadership style needs to be directive and that Liz's personality type is a High T. Bob takes the time to tell Liz how, when, and where the report is to be given. He reassures her by giving a detailed and structured explanation of the task. Liz feels comfortable because her need for control has been satisfied and Bob is sure that Liz understands what to do.

There is no implication here that *all* relationships or interactions of task assignments will be positive. However, the leader and follower must work toward the achievement of a positive power base for both.

LEAPFROG LEADERSHIP

One of the most confusing and frustrating problems with which a follower must deal is that of leader inconsistency. Whatever we believe about leadership behavior, "leapfrogging" from different styles without reason is unproductive. The key term here is "without reason." This would include, for example, a leader's yelling one moment and being kind the next. Even more subtly, though, would be a leader's using a coproducing leadership style with a follower on a specific task and then suddenly changing to the directing style. In one instance the leader is asking for suggestions and then, in the other starts telling the follower exactly what to do. Our whole approach in this text is to help leaders make reasonable decsions about the most effective leadership possible. Treating all followers the same may in itself be inconsistent based on personality, position, and leader style. We would not expect the same of a new company employee in comparison with an experienced one. The new employee must learn the ropes. The idea that leaders must treat followers the same has more to do with the legal requirements for equal opportunities than effective leadership. In fact, styles of leadership with the same employee may be different for different tasks.

Leapfrog leadership occurs when changes in the leadership approach and behavior take place without any perceived or real reason. It would also include changes in the leader's mood and attitude toward the follower. In addition, confusion is caused by problems in communication. In charting this type of leadership using the Power Management Model, one might see that a leader would assign a task using quadrant four leadership and regress later to using a quadrant one leadership style. This four to one leapfrog leadership style is inconsistent, to say the least. Let us say, for example, that Betty uses a trusting, quadrant four style with Sue when assigning a report to be typed, then checks on Sue every five minutes, using a quadrant one leadership style. Sue, feeling trusted at first, now is frustrated with her boss's change of behavior.

LEADER GUILT

Throughout the years, leadership theorists and developers have advocated their own brands of leadership. Many well-marketed commercial leadership development programs provide "the answer." The concepts of one best way to manage, situational leadership, and the participatory method have all espoused their own type of leadership. Sensitivity training, transactional analysis, script analysis, game analysis, and many more programs were each developed from a single point of view. For instance, after a two-week course on participatory management, Sam returns to his job. He tries to implement the new things he learned, but many problems begin to develop. Somehow his inexperienced staff doesn't understand how to participate and simply sits in the meetings without saying anything. Sam feels guilty because things don't work out.

There is always a danger not only in the bandwagon effect of any development program but also that a specific program will develop "leader guilt." Many times, for instance, guilt is felt when the leader uses a more directive style of leadership behavior that may at the time seem cold and impersonal. If the leader has only been trained to use a high human-relationship leadership style, there will be leader guilt. When a leader must use the quadrant one directing style but has been trained to use the democratic process, he or she feels guilty. Some situations or circumstances demand a more directive style from the leader. For instance, an army lieutenant will use quadrant one on the battlefield and other styles in less strenuous circumstances.

On the other hand, a leader who uses the wrong leadership

approach and knows better may feel "leader shame." There is a difference between calculating the best possible leadership procedure and then ignoring the evidence and thinking that only one leadership method will work. Say, for instance, that Bob is a trusted employee and is very capable of accomplishing this specific task. Bill, his boss, knows this but ignores that fact and proceeds to use the quadrant one leadership style. Bill knew better but wanted to put Bob in his place—not a very logical reason for using an inappropriate leadership style.

We owe it to ourselves as leaders to make the best use of the most up-to-date tools available when making decisions about people and events. This is what leadership development is all about. However, we also owe it to ourselves to be careful not to think that there is only one way to accomplish a task and lead a follower.

BUILDING EFFECTIVE LEADER BEHAVIOR

It is not enough for today's leader to decide between democratic and autocratic leadership behavior. The leader has many factors to consider in making a decision about the most productive leadership behavior to use. Several questions we should ask ourselves are:

1. What is the overall power position related to this specific task?
2. What power elements indicate some weakness in the power position?
3. What type of leadership behavior should be used as a result of the position analysis?
4. What are the personalities involved and how will they react to this assignment?
5. Will there be any possibility of negative power discrepancies as this assignment is made?
6. Will the leader/follower interaction result in more power for both parties?

The key to building effective leadership behavior is to have a procedure or process for making well-thought out and rational decisions. Making rational leadership decisions is not easy and takes practice. The leadership model discussed in the next chapter helps us develop a leadership language that will help us make our decisions more quickly, easily, and more effectively.

NOTES

1. Alfred Adler *Social Interest: A Challenge to Mankind* (London: Faber and Faber, 1938), pp. 72-73.

7
Power
Management Model

Effective leadership is a very complex process because it is so dependent on the circumstances, personalities, powers, and behaviors of the individuals involved. Our society can no longer, however, afford to develop only a few natural leaders who understand the process. Leadership must be studied by all who try to influence others. The leader in the United States must have a greater impact on performance, productivity, and organizational development if America is to keep up with the other developed nations of the world. The simple study of leadership is, however, not enough. For instance, we are told that leaders work hard. Does this mean the harder we work, the better leader we will be?

One of the problems with the study of power and leadership is that so many abstract theories and ideas are involved. How can the average business, governmental, or educational leader focus all of the abstract concepts into a practical and workable leadership tool? And how can this tool help leaders make more productive leadership decisions using simple and understandable steps? A road map, for example, is not the same as the real landscape but it is a good enough representation to be a very useful tool.

NEED FOR
COMMON LEADERSHIP LANGUAGE

Because leadership is so complex, there is a great need for a common understanding of the terms, concepts, and techniques involved. In other words, leaders need a common leadership language just as, for instance, programmers need a common computer language. This leadership language would help reduce the misunderstanding of leadership terms and concepts and would assist leaders in communicating more effectively about leadership problems. As it stands now, leaders must use terms such as *poor performance, incompetent, poor attitude, low-quality work,* and other emotionally charged terms. These terms are also confusing to followers as well as other leaders. It is almost as if the leader who uses the terms is relieved from analyzing the causes.

If such a common language could be developed, there would be a chance to reduce the emotional conflict that so often exists between leader and follower. Furthermore, the English language is filled with words and terms with several meanings, many of which have become emotionally charged. This compounds the problems of communication for the leader.

In recent years, the problem has been complicated by the many leadership development courses and programs that have come on the market using their own languages. The transfer of terms from one program to another is limited and costs the leadership student time, money, and effort to relearn. Unfortunately, this situation does not advance leadership development. For example, terms like *impoverished, maturity, participatory, situation, needs, incentives,* and so on have all taken on unique meanings depending on which leadership program is used.

In addition, leaders need a frame of reference for the various leadership theories. The graphic model has been somewhat useful in recent years in helping leaders visualize the leadership process. There is, however, a danger that any leadership model will be taken at face value. No model can describe all of the elements of effective leadership. Nevertheless, we need and desire a sense of perspective and some type of conceptual organization. To this end, the leadership language and graphic model become simply a tool and not the answer.

THE POWER MANAGEMENT MODEL

The Power Management Model presented in this chapter will provide the leader with a framework for making more productive decisions about people and events. The three parts of the model represent the three major fields of study in leadership-personality traits, circumstance-situational factors and specific leadership behaviors.

As James Owens said, "The best leadership style varies and depends on (a) the individual personality of the manager himself, (b) the individual followers, the kind of people they are and the kind of work they do, and (c) the particular situation and circumstances on any given day or hour."[1] The model helps us manage our leadership decisions in order to achieve the most powerful influence on events and people.

FIGURE 7-1. Power Management Model.

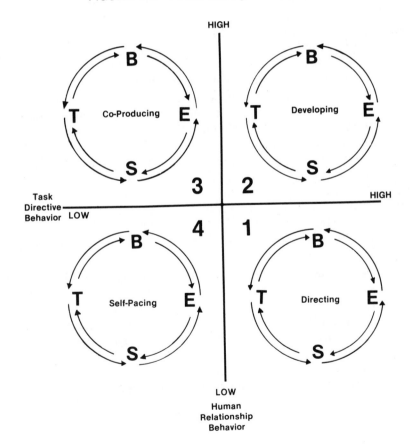

Based on the three major theories of leadership, the model should be viewed as having three dimensions:

1. **Position.** The position or circumstance determines what quadrant style the leader uses. For example, when we are in the position of leading in an uncertain environment with complex tasks, untrained staff, and so on, the degree of supervision will be high. In the second dimension, we recognize that there are different styles of leadership behavior and that task and relationship factors are part of that behavior. In this dimension, we determine what quadrant we must use to be an effective leader in our present position. This gives much more meaning to the kinds of leadership behaviors we use.

2. **Leadership Behavior.** Since there are various kinds of leadership behaviors, some organization of them is needed. The four styles in the Power Management Model have two features—task directive behavior and human relationship behavior. The task-directive behavior and human relationship behavior go from low to high. This creates four quadrants with each having a different mix of task directive and human relationship behavior by the leader. What behavior the leader uses depends on the position analysis described in Chapter 6. Because research has indicated that leadership behavior must change to meet the demands of the circumstances, the Power Management Model helps to organize this concept. For instance, we don't behave the same way when we have a poor position power as we do when we have a strong position power.

3. **Personality.** By knowing the personality type of each individual in our organization we can use more successful communications with each. For example, a High B will not always follow directions in the directing quadrant (Q1). This is important for us to know in order to more closely supervise the B's initial performance. Research tells us that personality is a factor in leadership and that the follower's personality is also important in the organization. Because of this, the Power Management Model provides this third dimension for the leader to consider.

Before progressing, one must understand a few things about the construction of the model. Leadership behavior is signified in the model by the descriptive terms in each quadrant: Q1—Directing, Q2—Developing, Q3—Coproducing, and Q4—Self-pacing. Note that there are no outside "walls" to the quadrants. This implies that the model should be used as a tool and that no model can neatly box in all the factors in leadership. In addition, the circles inside each quadrant represent the dynamic nature of the personality types the leader faces. The B, E, S, and T in each quadrant stand for the four types of personality.

USING THE MODEL

The crossed lines in the model represent the two major leadership factors in the assignment of a task—the task itself and human relations. As mentioned earlier, the four quadrants which result from the crossed lines indicate the different mixes of task directive behavior and human relationship behavior. For example, quadrant one (Q1) is high on task directive behavior and low on human relationship behavior. The behaviors described are those of the leader.

The three steps in the decision-making process using the model are:

1. Use the position analysis of all power elements to determine the overall power position. This will indicate the degree of supervision needed under the circumstances.

2. Identify the leadership behavior that is best under the circumstances in a given quadrant in the model (Directing, Developing, Coproducing, and Self-pacing).

3. Determine the type of personality of the follower and what effect that will have on the leadership approach.

For instance, let us say that Al is the supervisor in an auto repair shop. A car is brought in to be repaired, and Al must decide which mechanic gets the job. He analyzes who has the resources, training, time, motivation, and so on to do the repair. When he makes his selection, the style of leadership he uses with the mechanic is dictated by his analysis. If the mechanic has plenty of resources, training time, and motivation, he will use less supervision and the self-pacing style of leadership. On the other hand, the degree of directing supervision will increase as the power elements decrease. Al's final approach to the mechanic is based on the individual's personality. Al may need to spend more time explaining the standards and quality expected with a High B than he does with a High T personality.

Nevertheless, by using the three steps of the power management model, we can make more productive leadership decisions. The model makes this process easy because it gives us a picture of decisions to be made for effective leadership.

LEADERSHIP BEHAVIORS

Each quadrant in the Power Management Model calls for a different style or mode of leadership. There are certain leadership behaviors in each. Remember that our positions or circumstance determines what leadership style we use.

Directive (Q1)

This style is high in task or directing behavior on the part of the leader. The leader has determined that a high degree of supervision is needed under these circumstances and will tell the individual or group not only what to do but also how, when, and where to do the specific tasks.

While this leadership style calls for high task directive behavior, some human relationship behavior does exist. We are always trying to preserve good interpersonal relations even though some leaders will use the directive mode as an excuse to yell at followers. Most of the time yelling is neither useful nor necessary.

At this point, the leader is using directive behavior for another reason—to explore the potential of the follower. Can he or she follow directions? Does he or she have the basic ability to do the task? How much time will it take to train this individual? We are preparing the follower to move to quadrant two while at the same time gathering information about him or her that will be useful during the Developing (Q2) mode. One of the more interesting factors about human abilities is that a person may perform one task very effectively and another very poorly. We cannot assume that even the most trusted and experienced follower will perform all tasks at the same high level. Consequently, the leader constantly observes the potential as well as the ability of the follower.

For instance, an individual may be very good at writing letters but not reports. We see this kind of ability difference in the area of word processing where highly technical skills are needed. Performance on one type of equipment may not transfer to another. The point is that the leader should not assume that the ability to perform one task will carry over to another.

Developing (Q2)

In this quadrant, the leader uses a high degree of task and human relationship behavior. The leader has found that the individual or group has to have the ability to do the task and be ready for further training and development. The leader is developing the individual to take on more responsibility; therefore, a high relationship style is needed and means that the leader not only tells the follower how, when, what, and where but also *why*.

True training, at some point, must have a high degree of human relationship behavior and task directive behavior. Two-way communications must develop. The leader not only tells how, when, what, where, and why, but gives followers or subordinates an opportunity to ask questions about how, when, what, where, and why. Subordinates can accept more responsibility only when they are well-trained and informed.

In quadrant two, the leader is in control of the task decisions, and there is still a high degree of supervision. However, the leader is developing followers to be more self-directive when they progress to quadrants three and four. To do this, subordinates must be trained.

The concept of training and development is broader than the classroom experience. It can take place in many forms and in many ways. In a sense, the leader becomes the follower's mentor. The relationship must be developed to the point that the follower is not hesitant to ask questions about the assignments and thus learn more of the reasons behind the operation of the organization.

Coproducing (Q3)

The individual or group we are leading in this instance has above-average training, motivation, information, resources, and so on to complete the task. In addition, we feel that he or she can make a contribution to the decision-making process. Coproducing is the descriptive term selected for this quadrant because it implies a sharing of responsibility between the follower and the leader. When we feel that the individual can help solve production and performance problems, we use quadrant three.

The process of coproducing can be very formal. The Quality Circle movement in the United States is based on the coproducing or participatory management system. The Japanese have formalized the Quality Circle movement with great success. The Quality Circle is a group of people who voluntarily meet together on a regular basis to identify, analyze, and solve quality and other problems in their work area. The people described in the definition include workers *and* management.

The Quality Circle movement sounds simple, is easy to understand, and, on the surface, is effective. However, a major factor in the sixty percent failure rate of this movement is the lack of preparation and training of followers to constructively contribute to the process. The model described in this chapter can serve as a guide in developing followers to the point that they can accept the added responsibility of participating in management/productivity decisions. Individuals or groups should be moved from quadrant one (Directing) through quadrant two (Developing) before going to the Coproducing quadrant.

Self-Pacing (Q4)

Quadrant four is used when the individual or group has cultivated the leader's confidence and can complete at least ninety percent of the task without help. At this point, we can allow the follower to self-pace his or her own work. Again, we use position analysis to determine the leadership style to use. Remember that the key to this style (self-pacing) is confidence and that the individuals must perceive our confidence in them.

What should we expect of followers in quadrant four? The authors recommend a process called "completed staff work." Completed staff work is when the subordinate or follower identifies the problems connected with a task and proposes the solutions for the leader's approval or disapproval. This is consistent with the self-pacing leadership style described in quadrant four.

The words "completed staff work" are emphasized because the greater the difficulty of the task, the greater the tendency for the follower to present the work to the leader in piecemeal fashion. In quadrant four, the follower must work out the details, and he or she should not consult with the leader in the determination of those details no matter how perplexing they may be. Of course, this does not preclude consultation with the leader to obtain clarification or guidance essential to a constructive effort. He or she may and should consult other staff members. The product, whether it involves the pronouncement of a new policy or affects an established one, should be in final form when presented for approval or disapproval.

The concept of completed staff work may result in more work for the follower, but it results in more freedom for the leader. This is as it should be. Further, it accomplishes two things:

First, the decision maker is protected from incomplete ideas, voluminous memoranda, and immature oral presentations.

Second, the follower who has a real idea to sell is enabled to find a market more readily.

When a subordinate has completed the work, the final test for the follower is to ask, "If I were the decision maker, would I be willing to sign the paper I have prepared and stake my professional reputation on its being right?" If the answer is negative, the follower should take it back and work it over because it is not yet completed staff work.

If subordinates have the training, motivation, resources and time to do this specific project or task, completed staff work should be expected. However, we should express our trust and confidence to the individual that he or she can do the job. For the leader, completed staff work can be true delegation and not just abdication.

LEADERSHIP-STYLE LANGUAGE

The classification of each style of leadership in the model gives us the opportunity to use symbols in place of complicated style descriptions. For instance, we can now explain that we are using a Q4 style with a follower. In this one symbol, we have communicated how strong a position the follower is in, how we feel about his or her past performance, and how we intend to behave toward the follower when assigning a specific task. In addition, we have an indication of the type of relationship needed. As an example, a Q3 leadership behavior will be high in human relationship behavior and low in task directive behavior. On the other hand, a Q1 leadership style is low in human relationship behavior and high in task directive behavior. Consequently, the leadership style language enables us to reduce the amount of communication needed to convey great amounts of leadership information.

THE POWER CYCLE AND THE MODEL

In Chapter 6, we learned of the power cycle and how it related to our power base development with specific tasks and how the power cycle is comparable to the human life cycle. The power cycle concept gives another dimension to the Power Management Model and helps us understand how individuals gain and lose power between quadrants. However, the purpose of this review of the power cycle is to develop an understanding of how the leadership styles described in the model facilitate the power cycle development process for the followers. We will also explore what happens when negative leadership is used (Figure 7-2).

As we can see, the leadership styles in the power management model closely relate to the psychological and ability growth phases of the human being. For instance, the Q1 leadership style in the model corresponds to level one in the development of the fol-

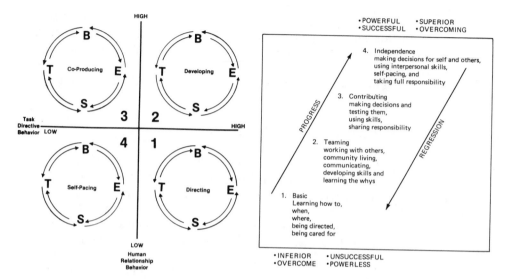

FIGURE 7-2. Power Management/Power Cycle.

lower's power base. The leader is in a directive style because of the analysis of the power elements, and the follower is in the Basic level of the power cycle because of developmental needs.

Most followers will make realistic evaluations of themselves in a situation and place their developmental level realistically on the power cycle. When the proper leadership approach is used with the appropriate power cycle level of the follower, a comfortable and productive relationship is established. However, our social norms will not always allow us to admit our weaknesses in a situation. Consequently, the leader must be perceptive and help the follower express true concerns about the task assignment. Let us say, for example, that Jim wants to impress his boss. Betty, who is Jim's boss, wants things to go well. That is, she doesn't want Jim to express concerns or identify problems in the work to be done. She has placed Jim in a position where success will be more difficult or even impossible. On the other hand, had Betty shown appreciation for Jim's concerns, many performance problems could have been avoided. It is even possible that Betty could have learned something from the honest exchange.

Again, we as leaders must analyze each follower, each task, and each set of circumstances because there is continuous movement between power and powerlessness from situation to situation. When we help the follower (or ourselves) with the process of gaining power, it is a step toward self-affirmation. As self-affirmation increases, performance improves.

The reasons for not progressing up the power cycle are infinite. Thousands of books have been written on why people fail, the effects of the loss of power, and why people stop or regress in their psychological development. The results of the loss of power can be aggression, violence, hostility, anxiety, apathy, and suspicion. Take Betty and Jim as an example. When Betty refuses to listen to Jim's concerns, she creates frustration and anxiety in Jim. He feels a loss of power over the situation, and, over time, a great deal of emotional conflict will result.

While it is not the purpose of this text to explore the causes and reasons for abnormal behavior, every leader must have some understanding for the possibility of emotional conflict caused by task assignments. The results of not understanding may be higher turnover, absenteeism, and unproductive behavior.

NEGATIVE POWER DISCREPANCIES AND THE MODEL

Every exchange between two people affects each individual's power base. A positive exchange occurs when each of the two power bases is maintained or expanded. A negative exchange occurs when one power base is expanded and the other reduced. The latter is more likely to be the case in leader/follower relationships. The leader has the opportunity to make an infinite number of positive exchanges but is limited in the number of negative exchanges before the relationship is destroyed. In other words, the leader cannot afford to provoke the follower to anger, frustration, or anxiety for very long before the follower quits or stops performing. In addition, the leader who follows this path stands the chance of having the follower transfer his or her anger and frustration to other followers. This could undermine the whole leadership process in the organization.

Every exchange between leader and subordinate is to maintain or acquire power. For instance, the act of yelling at a follower is a negative exchange. One individual's power base is expanded and the other's reduced. Effective leaders are in the business of helping followers build their power bases; only when this occurs will there be a stronger collective community power base.

As was discussed in Chapter 6, the negative use of power by the leader as well as by the follower causes a negative power discrepancy. We can learn how to analyze and correct negative power discrepancies by using the Power Management Model. We can classify negative power discrepancies as follows:

Negative Power Discrepancies Classification

0	=	No power discrepancy (positive relationship)
−1	=	The interaction is one quadrant off either way
−2	=	The interaction is two quadrants off
−3	=	The interaction is three quadrants off

When the leader, using the Power Management Model as a guide, assigns a task to a follower and both power bases are enhanced or at least maintained, there is no power discrepancy. If, however, the leader uses a Q4 approach and the follower is in Q1, there is a negative power discrepancy of −3. The consequences of the constant use of negative power interactions are as follows:

−1	=	Anxiety
−2	=	Frustration
−3	=	Aggression or apathy

In a work situation, for example, let us say that Jill is making an assignment to Howard and she is using a very direct (Q1) style. She continues to tell Howard what to do as well as how, where, and when to do the task. However, Howard has performed this specific task many times before with great success (Q4). Evidently Howard has all of the power elements to continue his high performance, yet Jill does not seem to recognize this fact. Jill has created a −3 Negative Power Deviation which is unnecessary and if continued, will cause aggressive or apathetic behavior on the part of Howard.

How does the leader cause a negative power discrepancy? The following questions should be asked by the leader:

1. Was the task assignment understood by the leader?
2. Were the power elements in the follower position taken into consideration?
3. Was the follower's power cycle level reviewed?
4. Was the right leadership style used?
5. Was the personality style of the follower taken into consideration?
6. Was the power base of the follower preserved or enhanced?

It may be, however, that the follower causes a negative power discrepancy. While we cannot assume that all performance problems are the fault of the leader, it is the responsibility of the leader to help the follower overcome such problems.

How does the follower cause a negative power discrepancy? The following questions should be asked:

1. Did the follower have an objective view of his or her power cycle level?
2. Did the follower understand the task assignment?
3. Does the follower have the wrong expectation of the goals of the organization?
4. Does the follower understand and make adjustments for the personality type of the leader?
5. Does the follower understand and make adjustments because of personality types?

The use of personal and position power is a struggle for significance, recognition, and achievement by the leader and by the follower. When the relationship between the leader and follower is positive, then the struggle advances. However, when there is a negative power discrepancy, both parties' power bases actually are diminished. The leader's responsibility is to fine tune the relationship.

USING THE LEADERSHIP LANGUAGE
OF THE POWER MANAGEMENT MODEL

As mentioned previously, we cannot remember all of the possible leadership variables for effective leadership. This is why leadership models are devised. The Power Management Model reminds us of the factors to consider such as position, style, and personality. With practice, a leader should be able to analyze what leadership approach to take in just a few seconds.

It is not difficult to understand how a leadership language can be developed out of the Power Management Model. When we are able to substitute one symbol for great amounts of information, we have a unique way of communicating and a new language. For instance, when the Power Management Model is understood, the following statements can easily communicate a world of information. "After PA, I used Q3 with a B and got 0 results." This would mean that after the leader used the Position Analysis, he or she used a quadrant three (coproducing) leadership style with a follower with a Bold personality and the results were very positive. The task assignment for the leader and follower was a comfortable one, and the power base of each was either maintained or enhanced. "When I used Q1 on a T there was a −3 NPD." This would mean, on the other hand, that the leader used a directive (Q1) style of leadership with a follower who had a Technical type personality and the results were a −3 negative power deviation. The implications of the remark would also be that the leader should have been in quadrant four (Self-pacing). In addition, this would indicate that the follower had the capability of performing at a higher level.

Let us review the leadership language we have established in this text with the Power Management Model:

Symbol	Concept
PA	Position Analysis
	Personality Types
B	Bold Personality Type
E	Expressive Personality Type
S	Sympathetic Personality Type
T	Technical Personality Type
	Leadership Behaviors
Q1	Directing leader approach or style
Q2	Developing leader approach or style
Q3	Coproducing leader approach or style
Q4	Self-pacing leader approach or style
	Power Interactions
0	Positive leader/follower interaction
NPD	Negative Power Discrepancy
−1	One quadrant NPD
−2	Two quadrant NPD
−3	Three quadrant NPD
	Power Cycle Levels
PC	Power cycle
PC1	Basic level
PC2	Teaming Level
PC3	Contributing Level
PC4	Independence Level
	Environmental Characteristics of Organizations
A/C	Active/Competitive
P/I	Persuasive/Interaction
W/S	Willing/Stable
P/S	Precise/Systematic

Because leadership involves human interactions, it is a very complex process. In order to get a grasp on the process, leaders need to analyze and code decision-making variables into a leadership language. This becomes more vital as our society becomes more diversified and technical. The leadership model and resulting language advocated in this text are the result of the three major leadership theories developed over the past 80 years. It is time for all types of leaders to take advantage of this research and become effective leaders.

When we bring all of the components of the Power Management Model and leadership language together, we are ready to make productive leadership decisions. Figure 7-3 is a composite of the Position Analysis and model and gives the leader a total view of all of

FIGURE 7-3. Leadership Action Plan.

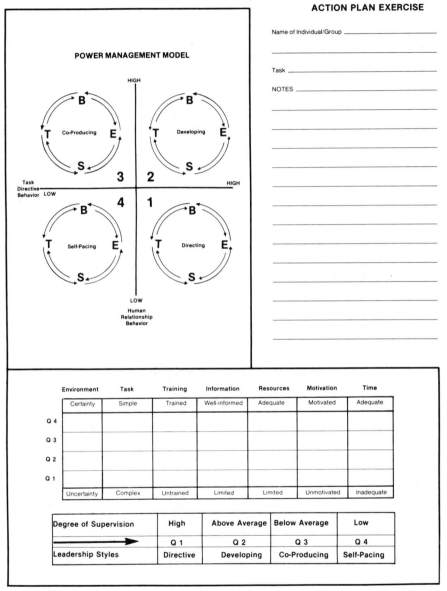

the factors of the leadership process. This composite becomes an action planning device for leaders.

Let us consider the following scene where the leader, Eric Hunter, is making an assignment to Jean Rhodes to complete the department budget.

JEAN: You wanted to see me, Mr. Hunter?

ERIC: Yes, Jean, come in, budget time. Need yours in next week. Here's what I want . . .

JEAN: That's OK. I know the procedure. Same as last year, right?

ERIC: Right. First, do a summary of this year's expenditures. You'll get that from the monthly printouts.

JEAN: I know, I reviewed them every month as they came out. I've already done that step.

ERIC: Then move on to step 2. Note changes in operations.

JEAN: This is all the same as before. And last year I had no problems.

ERIC: Then move on to step 3. Projections of coming operational requirements.

JEAN: Look, I know this stuff.

ERIC: Capital expenditures aren't the same as operational. Note that.

JEAN: As always—sure. What's the big deal here? I can handle this OK. Trust me! Please.

ERIC: Just going over it for you. I want it done right. On time. No screw-ups. Understand?

JEAN: Yes, SIR.

When we analyze the interaction, we can assume that the leader, Eric, is a High B using a Q1 leadership style. Jean, who has done the budget before, is in Q4 and has a High S personality.

Eric seemed to want quick results and used a very direct style. Because he uses a Q1 leadership style and Jean is in Q4, there is NPD of -3. Jean displays a little aggression in her conversation because of the discrepancy.

The Leadership Action Plan (Figure 7-3) can help prevent this type of negative power exchange. The exercise helps leaders analyze beforehand the appropriate leadership approach when assigning a task.

Consider the following interaction of Bob Hall, a janitor, and his boss David Jasper:

BOB: Evening, Mr. Jasper. (Mopping hallway) Everything go OK on the day shift?

DAVID: Evening, Bob. Yes, a good day. Glad it's over though. (Walks by, stops, looks at floor) Bob, you missed this area.

BOB: No, sir, I'll be getting that in a minute.

DAVID: Well, you know how to do the job, but if you would start from this corner, the doorway could be kept clear longer. Rules say we should keep exit doors clear.

BOB: Yes, sir, but I can do it faster starting down here. See, it sets me up to go down the next corridor without backtracking.

DAVID: Maybe, but it sure can cause congestion at the door. By the way, what type detergent are you using?

BOB: Standard supply.

DAVID: Good. What proportions do you mix it?

BOB: Like the box says. 4 to 1.

DAVID: Here on this surface my standard is 3 to 1 which is better. Doesn't leave a film. Use that next time. And try starting over there. It's worth a try, don't you think?

BOB: OK. (David Jasper leaves.) Been here five years. I know more than he does! Why won't he let me do my job? I never can understand why they promote guys who don't know how to do the work and won't let those who do know get on with the job!

It is obvious that there is a great deal of frustration on Bob's part as a result of the exchange. Bob has been doing a good job with the floors and is experienced at it. Bob is at the Q4 level, and David treats him as though he was at Q2. David's behavior could be part of his High T personality and this conflicts with Bob's High B personality. Because of this exchange, there was a −2 NPD and the result for Bob is frustration.

Leaders need to delegate tasks to followers and, whenever their development allows, let them do it. Remember, being allowed to do a task alone at the Q4 level is a motivator.

There are times, of course, that followers create the NPD. This sometimes happens when the follower wants independence too soon. Consider the following scene:

JACK: Richard, I'm really glad to have you working on this paper with me. Even though this is your first such assignment, I'm glad to have you on the team. Our stance on this will set the stage for everything we do in the next five years. So . . . well, I don't have to go on about its importance.

RICHARD: I won't let you down. I've jotted down an outline and . . .

JACK: Now, Dick, before we go any further, I think we should talk philosophy on this—you've not been here long and well, I think a feel for the flow of the organization is the key. What do you think?

RICHARD: I'll research that, too—let's move on.

JACK: What do you think though? What are your ideas? Let's build this together.

RICHARD: What's the matter? Don't you trust me? If you don't think I can do it, you're free to assign it elsewhere.

JACK: Now, don't be upset. Sure I trust you. Let's put this together as a team. How can we best get our message across?

RICHARD: We'll do it effectively. And I don't mean to sound presumptuous, but we won't get it done at all unless we stop talking and I'm given a chance to get on with it.

In this case, the leader, Jack, used the Q3 leadership style and the follower wanted to be in Q4. However, considering Richard has never done this type of report before, he should start in Q1. Consequently, both the leader and follower are in inappropriate quadrants.

It is up to the leader in this case to adjust the expectations of the follower—that is, to show how difficult it will be to do the task without a thorough understanding. While in the scene there is an NPD of −1, the problem is more serious because both parties are on the wrong level.

SUMMARY

One of the problems that has plagued leadership development in the past is the complex human behaviors we described in complex systems. There was the need for a tool or language that would help leaders focus their attention on productive leadership decisions. The leadership theorists, scholars, researchers, and others in the past have demonstrated their genius in exploring the intricacies of the leadership process. However, the act of true genius would be to move all of the abstract knowledge about leadership into a practical tool for the common man.

The danger, of course, is that simple leadership tools will be used as an end and not as a means. It is the organization of thought, the analysis of factors, the understanding of common terms, and the practice of new leadership skills that bring positive leadership power to life. The Power Management Model becomes of value in this process.

NOTES

1. James Owens, "A Reappraisal of Leadership Theory and Training," *Personnel Administrator*, Nov. 1981, p. 84.

8

Power Communications

One of the most important and basic elements of human behavior is communication. The process of thought expresses itself through nonverbal, verbal, interpersonal, and intrapersonal communications. Effective communication is at the very heart of power management and productive leadership. The leader who is intelligent, talented, and a good problem solver can fail because of poor communications. It is not enough to have the solution to a problem. That solution must be conveyed to others in a convincing and compelling manner. The follower must be influenced to perform not just at a minimum level but at maximum productivity.

Far too many leaders think that communication is simple—that telling followers what to do means that organizational goals will be achieved. However, productive communication takes place only when the leader is sensitive to the emotional, personal, and power cycle status needs of the individual. Communication is a two-way process in which the effective leader receives and gives information, whereas ineffective leadership is compounded by the lack of communication with others in the organization. Many an organization has failed because the leader did not understand what was actually going on. Leaders can set themselves up to fail by cutting off true communications and using only the directive (Q1) style of leadership.

PROBLEMS IN COMMUNICATION

There are many false assumptions about communication which are held by leaders. Here are a few:

1. **When we explain a task assignment one time to a follower, he or she understands.** It is unrealistic for a follower to grasp the total assignment with only one explanation. Many times the actual performance of a task uncovers questions of procedure, quality standards, or the lack of essential information that even the leader could not anticipate. In addition, assignments are sometimes made under emotional conditions that block comprehension.

2. **Written communications (memos) mean that followers will understand the task assignment or procedure.** The English language is not simple. Words have many meanings; anyone who has written a memo knows this. The written message we think we have conveyed may not be what the follower receives.

3. **Long explanations of complex ideas mean the follower will understand.** The average person can remember only five specific pieces of information at a time. That is to say, followers need time to learn and absorb complex information. The leader who gives long and detailed information about task assignments without allowing the follower to absorb it completely will be disappointed. Moreover, learning is not just hearing.

4. **Using jargon will facilitate follower understanding.** The falseness of this assumption is self-evident. Yet, it is amazing how many leaders continue to use little-understood terms with followers. The reason is most likely that the leader feels more powerful when jargon is used. This, of course, is a false perception of many leaders.

5. **Communication is unemotional.** This false assumption is again most often the perception of the leader. When the leader makes an assignment, there is always an emotional dimension with the follower. The emotion can be positive or negative (a gain or loss of power) or perceived as such by the follower. Moreover, the emotional aspect of meeting with the leader does not necessarily diminish over time.

6. **Listening is easy.** Nichols points out the problems with this assumption:

> "On the average in America we talk one hundred twenty-five words per minute; but if you put a man up in front of an audience and get that degree of formality in the situation that always ensues when he starts speaking informatively or instructionally to a group seated before him, he slows down. In America we average one hundred words per minute when we speak informatively to an audience. How fast do people out front listen? Or, to put it more accurately, how fast do listeners think in words per minute when they listen? We know from three different studies that you will never face. an audience of any size at all that does not think at an easy cruising speed of four hundred to five hundred words per minute. The difference between speech speed and thought speed operates as a tremendous pitfall. It is a snare and a delusion. It is a breeder of false security, and a breeder of mental tangents."[1]

7. **Communication is the same in all settings.** The same message by the leader delivered when behind a desk, when standing, or when out in the hall will not be perceived the same way by the follower. The leader must understand that the setting for the communication has an impact on how it will be received.

8. **Communications of task assignments should be the same for all followers.** The leader's communications approach is dependent on the personality type of the follower. For instance, some people need more specific information than others in order to feel comfortable with the assignment. Personality types dictate the style of communication which should be used.

Whether or not leadership communication is effective depends on many factors. When the leader communicates a task assignment to the follower, it sets in motion a process in the recipient that may or may not have the desired results. Perceptive leaders will learn how to overcome obstacles in communications. The story is told of an incident that happened in a large utility company. A violent storm did extensive damage to utility lines in another part of the state, and crews were sent to start the repair work. During the course of the repair, a maintenance truck driver was called in by his supervisor. The supervisor handed a piece of paper to the driver and said, "Take this to Centerville the first thing in the morning."

The next morning the truck driver faithfully delivered the piece of paper to the crew foreman 150 miles away at Centerville. As the driver turned to leave, the crew foreman asked, "Where is the stuff? "What stuff?" said the driver. "The equipment, material, and supplies listed on this paper!" exclaimed the foreman.

The truck driver's supervisor had not made clear the task assignment, and the driver had not bothered to read the list on the paper. One working day had been lost for an entire repair crew because of poor communications.

COMMUNICATION STYLES

The effectiveness of our leadership depends on how we communicate with others. One important dimension of the communication process is style. The mode, style, or tone of the leader's communication to followers is a result of the leader's personality type. As was discussed in Chapter 5, our personality type guides our behavior. Most of the time, the average leader is unaware of how his or her personality is expressed when communicating with others. When we consider the B.E.S.T. personality types, we realize that each has a style of communication.

Taking into consideration each personality type, we can make the following observations about communication styles:

1. **The Bold personality uses the direct style.** In communicating with others, the Bold personality type likes to feel in charge of the conversation. Because the Bold likes challenges, quick action, and problem solving, his or her conversation tends to be direct and short. The Bold can appear to be very decisive and may even appear to be blunt. The conversation may tend to be one-way, and the Bold individual is often accused of not listening because of it. The Bold's conversation reflects a personality type which needs independence, power, freedom, and quick results.

An extreme example of a High B is General George Patton. Because of his directness, there was no doubt how he felt. On more than one occasion, the General found himself in trouble with other officers and with the press. While this communication style served him well on occasions, it almost destroyed his career.

2. **The Expressive personality uses the talkative style.** The Expressive type likes to feel power through a persuasive style. Persuading others to his or her point of view by talking to them makes the Expressive type feel successful. The Expressive type likes to be around people, to be popular with

them, and to appear successful to them. The High E likes to be optimistic and gives the impression of being very positive. On the other hand, the Expressive type may tend to talk too much, not be very objective about work to be done, and may oversell ideas. The High E's conversation is a function of wanting to be popular and influential, to be accepted, and to gain public recognition.

The High E uses word pictures in conversation and likes to perform before others. Most effective salespeople are High Es because of their ability to persuade with words. Moreover, effective teachers, politicians, and actors tend to be Expressive individuals.

3. **The Sympathetic personality uses the sincere style.** In communicating with others, the Sympathetic type likes to be sincere. The Sympathetic type needs to feel appreciated and finds that feeling as a member of a group. However, the High S's conversation will reflect a desire for stability in the environment and because of that desire, the individual will respond slowly to new situations. While he or she is turned off by an aggressive person, he or she does respond to those who give personal attention and appreciation. The High S is a sympathetic listener because he or she likes to feel needed.

If asked to make a presentation, the High S may be rather matter-of-fact and colorless. While using the sincere style, the High S tends toward calm and nonaggressive language.

4. **The Technical personality uses the organized style.** The High T type uses terms like *how, when* and *where* in conversation. They like to feel that things are organized, logical, and detailed. The technical personality finds security in a low-risk, organized, and cooperative environment which uses standard operating procedures.

Conversation with High Ts are typified by details and the desire to maintain quality. The High T's communication is a function of wanting order, control, and organization in the environment. It is almost as if the High T is communicating like an engineer. The aim is always to build a framework of order, logic, and organization into the communications. Felix Unger of "The Odd Couple" was a very High T. This movie and TV character was obsessed with cleanliness, order, quality, and neatness.

There is both the potential for excellent teamwork and for

much conflict in the interaction between two or more personality types. The leader must take into consideration the personality type of the follower as well as his or her own personality type when forming committees or teams. One can imagine what would happen if one person wants quick results and the other seeks more precise information. Regardless of which type is the leader or follower, the chances are that these two personality types will have conflicts unless they understand each other's style. In fact, the High B and the High T team combination can be very productive because the High B can imagine how to solve problems in new ways and the High T can monitor the quality of the new approach.

COMMUNICATIONS STYLE
AND FOLLOWER PERCEPTION

Much of the impression and response a follower will have about the leader's effectiveness comes from the leader's communication style. The direct style on the part of the leader can be mistaken for harshness or bluntness. The talkative style leader can lead followers to believe there is no urgency for the task to be accomplished. When leaders and followers do not understand the different types of personalities and their strengths and weaknesses, personality conflicts will inevitably result. Personality conflicts are on a day-to-day basis and are the number one problem in any organization.

The perceptive leader will understand his or her own communication style and what effect it has on followers, and the positive leader/follower relationship will be preserved. Unperceptive leaders or leaders who don't care what effect they have on followers are called "stress carriers" because every interaction they have with followers creates stress. If the leader is constantly moving around in the organization asking why things have not been done, followers will feel pressure and frustration. This is particularly true when leaders work in very close proximity to the follower because the leader is not only looking at the progress being made but also at the methods used by the follower to accomplish the task.

However, when followers are in another location, say another building or even another state, the follower feels less stress to conform to the time schedule and methodology of the leader. Communications about tasks are judged more on results than methods. Moreover, when followers see their leader as a resource for positive and helpful communications, their productive behavior is reinforced.

THE POWER MANAGEMENT MODEL
AS A COMMUNICATIONS SYSTEM

We tend to use words and language as a substitute for real objects because it is easier for us to code ideas in the thought process. Communication is a complicated process which theorists have tried to reduce into a model. Using the traditional communication model, Figure 8-1 shows the elements of communication in the Power Management Model.

FIGURE 8-1. Power Management Communications Systems.

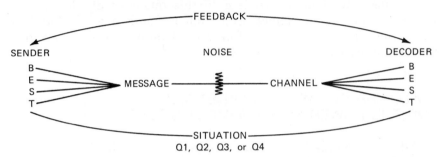

As the model indicates, the leader's style of communication depends on his or her personality type. As we have discussed, the tone, texture, and kind of communication for each type will be different. The sender's message goes through some type of channel—memo, verbal, nonverbal, and so on—and is received by the decoder with his or her respective personality type. For example, if a High E sends a message and a High B receives it, there may be a different interpretation based simply on personality type. Let us say that Bill is a High E, and he tells Joe, a High B, to be on the lookout for an additional clerical assistant. Joe interprets the message in more concrete terms and hires the new assistant.

Each message has internal or external interference. For instance, anxiety or preoccupation are forms of internal interference, in contrast to noises from an air conditioner, fan, or dripping water that are forms of external interference. Anything that draws attention away from the message is noise.

The situation or circumstances in which the communication takes place between the leader and follower has an impact on the success of the exchange. Directing, developing, coproducing, and self-pacing leadership approaches are all actually modes of communication. When the appropriate quadrant is used, there is positive communication for both parties. And, as discussed previously, negative power deviations are caused by poor communications.

The most powerful communication the leader can use in this situation is to ask the follower to repeat the task assignment, check his or her work after a short period of time, and stress quality. This communication should, of course, be done in a positive way.

The Power Management Communications Model described above is simply a point of departure for picturing the flow of information. However, it can be used as a tool for analyzing communication problems, and the feedback received during the interaction between leader and follower helps to solve those problems. The leader needs to help the High E in this quadrant develop a time schedule and task objectives. The High E stands a good chance of being well-liked by his or her followers if he or she is perceived to be friendly *and* organized.

FOLLOWER COMMUNICATION STYLES AND THE POWER MANANGEMENT MODEL

In order to fine tune leadership power and communications, we must not only understand the four types of personalities but also how each type behaves in each quadrant of the model. The Catalogue of Follower Behavior Patterns which follows is a very useful tool in assisting the leader/subordinate communication process. The catalogue gives the leader an idea of how each personality type reacts to leadership in each quadrant. Note how a follower with one type of personality behaves differently when assigned a task in each of the four quadrants.

CATALOGUE OF FOLLOWER PATTERNS

Quadrant 1

Bold Follower Personality
with Directing Leader Style
(High Task–Low Relationship)
- Will not always ask for help
- Wants to do it even without understanding
- Needs direction and evaluation
- Does not always pay attention to details

- May react too quickly

The most powerful communication the leader can use in this situation is to ask the follower to repeat the task assignment, check his or her work after a short period of time, and stress quality. This communication should, of course, be done in a positive way.

Quadrant 2

Bold Follower Personality
with Developing Leadership Style
(High Task–High Relationship)

- May concentrate too much on task at the expense of others
- May want to direct others
- Will be open in dealing with others—too open
- May be too competitive with team members
- Likes clear objectives
- Likes to be assertive
- Likes risk

Point out to the follower his or her impact on others in this situation. Stress quality of work rather than competitiveness. Help the follower work as a member of the team.

Quadrant 3

Bold Follower Personality
with Coproducing Leadership Style
(High Relationship–Low Task)

- May want to do task alone
- May resent not being free to do own projects
- Will be straightforward
- Likes challenges
- Likes short meetings and quick results
- Needs authority
- May not prepare for meetings
- May fail to consult with others
- May try to become too authoritarian

Again stress how the follower must work with others so that decisions will be better. Help the follower learn positive communications skills and how to prepare for meetings.

Quadrant 4

Bold Follower Personality
with Self-pacing Leadership Style
(Low Task–Low Relationship)

- Likes low relationship—independence
- Likes being able to set own pace
- Likes challenge of freedom
- May overlook details
- Likes to keep busy
- Will be unaware of impact on others
- Will apply pressure
- Will assume responsibilities
- May make risky decisions
- May not get approval before acting

The follower should do well in this setting. However, the leader must take time to evaluate the following decisions in a constructive and positive way. Make sure the follower feels trusted.

Quadrant 1

Expressive Follower Personality
with Directing Leadership Style
(High Task–Low Relationship)

- Detail work may be frustrating
- Will be unaware of time
- May try to socialize too much
- May be too optimistic about ability to do job
- May let popularity get in way of doing task
- Will be enthusiastic
- Will be talkative
- Will be confident
- Will be outgoing
- Needs goals and objectives

If the assignment is detailed and there are long periods of working alone, this follower may have problems. The leader will need to help the follower with time management by clearly defining goals, objectives, and time limits.

Quadrant 2

*Expressive Follower Personality
with Developing Leadership Style
(High Task–High Relationship)*

- Will be good at getting along with others
- Will help others look on positive side
- Will try to gain popularity
- Will be a good spokesperson for group
- Will be able to persuade team members
- Likes to talk
- Likes to be neighborly
- May waste time talking
- May like to be with people at the expense of the task
- Will be trusting of others

The follower will communicate and work well in this quadrant because of its high relationship element. However, the urge to visit by the follower could be lessened by the leader's stressing time on task.

Quadrant 3

*Expressive Follower Personality
with Coproducing Leadership Style
(High Relationship–Low Task)*

- Likes to look successful
- Likes recognition
- Likes acceptance
- May be overly optimistic
- Needs goals and objectives
- May be persuasive without facts
- May want too many meetings
- May talk too much

Again, the follower may desire to visit, and the leader will need to press for decision-making ideas. The leader should also insist that the follower prepare beforehand for any coproducing activity. Some structure may still be needed even in Quadrant 3.

Quadrant 4

Expressive Follower Personality
with Self-pacing Leadership Style
(Low Task–Low Relationship)

- May be hard for leader to function without follower's support
- May have hard time managing own time
- May have hard time setting goals and objectives
- Likes to spend time with others
- May delay unpleasant decisions
- Dislikes working alone
- Will motivate people
- Needs to plan and concentrate on projects
- Needs to develop technical skills
- Needs to be more objective about self-pacing

The leader needs to help the High E in this quadrant develop a time schedule and task objectives. The High E in Q4, who is accepting more and more self-pacing responsibility, stands a good chance of being well-liked by his or her own followers if perceived to be organized as well as friendly.

Quadrant 1

Sympathetic Follower Personality
with Directing Leadership Style
(High Task–Low Relationship)

- Will need time to adjust to new task
- Will be willing
- Will be dependable
- Will be loyal
- Needs personal attention
- Needs understanding boss
- Will be a good producer
- Will listen
- May lack a sense of urgency
- May work for work's sake

The leader should be especially clear on what, when, how, and so on to this follower, and personal attention should be given by soft verbal comments. This follower may want to work overtime but should be discouraged unless it is necessary.

Quadrant 2

Sympathetic Follower Personality
with Developing Leadership style
(High Task–High Relationship)

- Will be amicable with others
- May become stubborn with high Bs
- May be possessive about doing own work
- May not communicate vital information to others
- May enjoy doing job himself or herself rather than with others
- Will have good technical skills but poor people skills
- Likes to be a member of a group
- Does not like change in group
- Will be low key in working with others
- Likes appreciation

This follower will be a good team member and will respect the leader's directions. However, he or she may feel more secure in a routine task than in working with others. The leader needs to help the follower learn how to communicate more dynamically with others.

Quadrant 3

Sympathetic Follower Personality
with Coproducing Leadership Style
(High Relationship–Low Task)

- Will be sincere
- Will be willing
- Will be dedicated
- May be too content in coproducing style
- May want to do work himself or herself, not to coproduce
- May feel loss of importance in coproducing
- May procrastinate
- May not like to help with decisions
- May neglect planning so that he or she can coproduce

The leader will need to draw out ideas from the High S follower. Since the follower is loyal, he or she may not feel any urgency in coproducing. The leader needs to communicate the follower's worth in the decision.

Quadrant 4

Sympathetic Follower Personality
with Self-pacing Leadership Style
(Low Task–Low Relationship)

- May feel no urgency to develop other people
- May be too lenient with passive subordinates
- May not like to make decisions for change
- May put off unpleasant decisions
- May lack a sense or urgency
- May be too patient
- May be too involved with status quo
- May be unable to apply pressure when needed
- May be inflexible
- May be unable to keep many projects going at same time

In self-pacing, this follower should be given specific task assignments to accomplish. He or she must feel supported by the leader particularly with unpleasant situations.

Quadrant 1

Technical Follower Personality
with Directing Leadership Style
(High Task–Low Relationship)

- Needs low-risk situation
- Needs a lot of explanation
- Needs organization
- Likes standards
- Needs encouragement
- Likes a logical approach
- Likes low-stress work
- May ask too many questions
- May check and recheck work already done

The follower must feel secure in the task assignment, and the leader should furnish written or oral details of the step-by-step procedure. Security is gained by communicating a sense of order.

Quadrant 2

Technical Follower Personality
with Developing Leadership Style
(High Task–High Relationship)

When working with others, the High T follower tends toward the task dimension of the quadrant. For well-rounded teams, this is vital. However, the others in the team must understand this. The leader can facilitate this teamwork by positive communication about the need for the High T's contribution to quality and details.

- Will avoid unpleasantness with others
- Likes to go by the book with others
- Likes regimentation
- May spend too much time on details
- May not trust others
- May not delegate anything to others
- Will be attentive to details
- May overdo planning before making decision
- May be too serious with others
- May be too cautious with others

Quadrant 3

Technical Follower Personality
with Coproducing Leadership Style
(High Relationship–Low Task)

- Will research and investigate
- Will be cooperative
- Will want justification
- May specialize too much
- Needs thinking time
- Needs standard operating procedures
- May be tense at times
- May be overly cautious in making joint decisions
- Will try to reduce risk in decisions

This High T follower will most likely be prepared with facts and be ready to coproduce. However, the leader must help the follower to see the "big picture" and that some details may have to be worked out in the process of time.

Quadrant 4

Technical Follower Personality
and Self-pacing Leadership Style
(Low Task–Low Relationship)

- May be tentative rather than firm
- May avoid risky decisions
- May tend to refer decisions back to leader
- May ask for more information than necessary
- May regiment his or her own followers
- May want perfection in form, procedure, and detail
- May be overly concerned about making mistakes
- May spend more time supervising than required
- Will not be creative in problem solving
- May not develop his or her followers

When this High T follower assumes the self-pacing mode as given by the leader, he or she will need to provide his or her own structure to the task assignment. That is, the High T follower who is given an assignment in quadrant four must decide when, what, why, and so on for himself or herself. The leader must be able to provide details at times to develop the security base needed by the High T follower in quadrant four.

COMMUNICATING TASK ASSIGNMENTS

The act of leadership implies that there is a goal in mind. It is not the purpose of this text to help leaders identify goals and objectives. It is, however, the purpose of *Power Management* to help leaders reach those identified goals and objectives. Consequently, the assigning of identified tasks becomes important to the power leadership process. Figure 8-2 gives the flow of task assigning and follow-up.

FIGURE 8-2. Task Assignment Process.

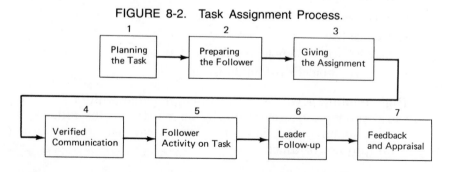

1. **Planning the Task.** Task assignments need to be well-thought out before the leader approaches the follower. What are the results the leader desires? What are the parts of the assignment? How long should it take? Does the follower have adequate power elements before starting? All of these questions need to be thought out before communicating the task to the follower.

2. **Preparing the Follower.** As we have seen, the various personality types react to communication in different ways. The leader should approach each type of personality with this in mind. For instance, a greater detailed description of the task to be done will be needed for a High T. The preparing of the follower then is dependent on the follower's previous experience, the power elements, and the follower's personality.

3. **Giving the Assignment.** The leader's communications should be clear and matter-of-fact. The order to accomplish a task is best given as one adult to another. The implication is that this reduces any misunderstanding because of negative emotions.

4. **Verifying Communication.** Leaders will save a lot of time if they ask the follower to repeat the task assignment. When this occurs, the leader is sure that the follower understands the task assignment and all of its implications. At this point, the leader has an opportunity to make sure that the follower does not go too far in the interpretation of the task assignment. That is, the follower, because he or she is the follower, may hang on every word the leader says and be apt to take the leader's directions as hard and cold. For example, if a leader was assigning a task using a quadrant three leadership style, the follower may perceive the assignment being given in the quadrant one style. The verifying of communication by the leader can help resolve any perceptual differences.

5. **Follower Activity on Task.** Having prepared the follower, given the assignment, and verified the communications, the leader must now give the follower time to accomplish the task. The follower must have the freedom to perform, use his or her skills, and produce the desired results. Leaders who stand over followers complicate matters for the follower and waste their own time.

6. **Leader Follow-up.** The leader should establish checkpoints during the progress of the assignment to make sure of the direction, quality, and time schedule. It is easier to have the follower redo parts of the project than it is to have the whole

project done again. Again, it is not necessary for the leader to stand over the follower, but it is advisable to check work in progress from time to time.

7. **Feedback and Appraisal.** High follower performance is very dependent on the feedback of the leader. Unfortunately, many leaders do not take the time to communicate about problems or even improvement in follower production. There are even systems of evaluation that take place only every six months. Many leaders are upset when problems arise in performance yet say nothing when high quality is maintained. Followers need constant feedback on the task and their performance. This includes good and poor performance.

The assignment of tasks takes place in the context of the position, personality, and leader behavior in a given situation. The communication of the task to the follower is often thought of as a simple process. This is not true—at least if high-quality performance is desired.

COMFORT ZONE

When the leadership style or approach being used with a subordinate or follower is appropriate, the result is usually a comfortable communication fit. The follower feels good in the way he or she is being led, and the leader feels better about the developing relationship. The leader can approach the "comfort zone" with a follower by:

1. Using the leadership style as dictated by the position analysis.
2. Increasing or maintaining the power of the follower.
3. Communicating according to the appropriate quadrant and follower personality style.
4. Rewarding open communications.
5. Listening actively.
6. Anticipating follower behavior because of personality type.
7. Having the follower paraphrase what is said about the task assignment.
8. Communicating as one adult to another.
9. Watching and responding to nonverbal cues—positive or negative.

SUMMARY

Communication is not easy. Leaders must be especially careful not to create problems and lower productivity because they do not take the time to plan communications. Leaders must be active communicators.

The Power Management Model described in this book, to a large degree, is a communication system. Personality, position, and leadership behavior help create the perceptions subordinates and followers have of leaders, and using the best fit of these factors will help build the personal and position power of the leader as well as that of the follower.

NOTES

1. Ralph G. Nichols, "Listening is Good Business," *Readings in Management,* 5th ed., ed. Max Richards (Cincinnati, Ohio: South-Western Publishing Co., 1978), p. 100

9

Power
Motivation

It has been said that people do things for their own reasons—that they are motivated by their own wants and needs. This is not entirely true. Often we are motivated by external and even internal powers of which we are not aware. Certainly at times we are coerced by external powers into doing things we do not like to do. While we may prefer to do otherwise, we are influenced by other powers that overrule our own personal preferences. Love, intellect, competition, and affiliation are also powers that can sweep us away from fulfilling our own personal wants and needs.

Influence is a form of power motivation that is centered around information. We are influenced by bits and pieces of information many times a day. As we learn and process this information, we are motivated to change our behavior. Going to school is an influencing process that persuades children to act differently. Even the more coercive rules of a school are instructive in nature and reflect how society as a whole deals with negative power. The rule against fighting, for example, restricts violent behavior between students but also teaches that fighting is bad. Other more subtle standards of performance can teach respect, ethics, etiquette, and criteria about quality.

This information serves as background for the positive use of power later in the adult world.

Power in an organization takes many forms. There are, for example, both internal and external powers that motivate followers to work toward organizational goals. The question in recent years has been "How can leaders create in followers a greater internal desire to increase productivity and performance?" Coercion as motivation has been decreasing, and the powers of love, intellect, competition, and affiliation have been on the increase in the modern organization.

In this chapter, we will explore how leaders can develop the followers' desire to work toward organizational goals. Several major motivational theories will be reviewed and related to the Power Management Model. The goal is to show leaders how they can influence followers to accomplish organizational tasks.

MAJOR THEORIES OF MOTIVATION

Dr. Abraham Maslow developed what he called a Hierarchy of Needs.[1] The premise is that higher levels of individual needs cannot be met until lower levels of needs have been satisfied. Thus, a hierarchy. The implication for motivation is that the leader cannot influence followers by helping them to fill higher level needs until lower level needs are met. For instance, recognizing the follower for good performance may be difficult when his or her house is on fire.

It is interesting to note the similarities between Maslow's hierarchy and the power cycle discussed earlier. If, as Alfred Adler suggests, the human struggle is from inferiority to superiority, then Maslow has categorized that struggle. We are all constantly moving up and down the hierarchy depending on the situation and the gain or loss of power. One moment we are doing something we like to do and the next we are trying to do something entirely new to us.

When we apply the hierarchy to the Power Management Model, we can find the following relationships:

Maslow's Follower Needs	Model Quadrants	Facilitative Leader Behavior
Survival	Quadrant 1	Directing
Safety and Security	Quadrant 1	Directing
Love and Belonging	Quadrant 2	Developing
Esteem	Quadrant 3	Coproducing
Self-actualization	Quadrant 4	Self-pacing

In looking at the relationship on a task-specific basis, it is the leader's responsibility to facilitate the filling of the follower's needs in each quadrant. For instance, if the follower's house were to burn, the leader can offer emotional security through verbal support and understanding. On the other hand, the leader can recognize another follower's mastery of a task assignment at the appropriate time, thus filling the follower's need for esteem. In other words, leader actions depend on the follower.

A classic theory of motivation was developed by Dr. Frederick Herzberg. After a series of major investigations, Herzberg concluded that the factors involved in producing motivation and job satisfaction are separate from the factors that produce job dissatisfaction.[2] These two factors are not opposites of each other. This is to say that removing a cause of dissatisfaction will not motivate employees but will only eliminate a state of dissatisfaction. True productivity and motivation can come only through the provision of those factors that lead to extreme job satisfaction.

Factors that Lead to Job Dissatisfaction	*Factors that Lead to Job Satisfaction*
Unfair policy and administration	Growth
Unfair supervision	Advancement
Relationships with supervisors	Responsibility
Working conditions	Pride in the work itself
Salary	Recognition
Relationships with peers	Achievement
Personal life	
Relationships with subordinates	
Status	
Security	

We can see how Herzberg's concepts apply to the Power Management Model. For example:

Herzberg Concepts	*Model Concepts*
Unfair supervision	Leader not in proper quadrant
Relationship with peers	Teaming personality types
Status	Using higher-order leadership behavior with subordinates
Security	Leader using Q1 to make subordinate feel secure at task
Growth	Q2 leader behavior

Advancement	Q3 and Q4 leader behavior
Responsibility	Q3 and Q4 leader behavior
Pride in the work itself	Praise from leader in all quadrants
Recognition	Q2, Q3, and Q4 leader behavior
Achievement	Q4 leader behavior

Both Maslow and Herzberg found that recognition was a high-order human need. In a real sense, the theory ascribed by B. F. Skinner on reinforcement is a model of how to apply recognition. Leaders who learn to use reinforcement techniques developed by Skinner will exert a more positive influence on the productivity of followers.[3]

According to Skinner, leaders should structure reinforcement systems that are contingent on specific productive behavior. Leaders should learn to modify a follower's behavior by giving him or her a sense of accomplishment, recognition, and praise when earned.

To increase the follower's performance motivation, the manager should:

1. State the specific job performance behavior that is desired.
2. Reinforce the desired behavior after it happens through praise and recognition.
3. Reinforce immediately (feedback).
4. Reinforce systematically by plan.

Let us say, for example, that it is important for a follower to keep an accurate record of the money in a cash register. If the accuracy rate is high, the leader gives some positive verbal comment to the follower. If, however, the accuracy level is low, the leader can then give positive verbal comments for improvement. It is important to remember that the recognition be given for the actual performance and not be generalizations.

MANIPULATIVE POWER

Here are just a few words about manipulative power. In the truest sense of the word, a parent who gives a child a piece of candy to stay out of the street or behave in the grocery store is manipulating that child. If, on the other hand, the same parent gave the child a piece of candy to shoplift in the grocery store, it would also be manipulation. In either case, the child is unaware of the reason for his or her behavior, only the results of it. Consequently, manipulation can be good or bad depending on who is doing the manipulating.

The ultimate aim of the Power Management Concept is to

have followers act in responsible and independent ways. The leader facilitates the growth of the follower up the power cycle and, at the same time, through each of the Power Management Model quadrants until the follower can self-pace his or her own behavior. No longer will the follower need to be manipulated to accomplish the task assignment. Again, the term *manipulate* has become a negative term. However, we all manipulate, influence, lead, persuade, and so on. Manipulation is simply the managing or influencing of another.

PRACTICAL APPLICATION OF MOTIVATIONAL THEORIES

Skinner's theory advocates the reinforcing of productive behavior. The pleasure one receives from the reinforcer becomes an incentive to continue the productive behavior. James F. Lincoln recognized the importance of this concept in his book *Incentive Management* written in 1951. He pointed out:

> Incentive management is not a so-called efficiency scheme alone. It is a philosophy of life and production that develops new aspirations and usefulness in all affected by it. Do not approach it from any other point of view. Incentive is not a way to get the worker to do more as an end in itself. It is a way to get him to be part of the economic team, on the excellence of which the future of our country depends. It is a way to get him to play the game in industry as a member of the economic team that has made America greater than any other nation, economically. It also opens a way toward fuller realization of the American dream and promise of a fuller, richer, happier, better life for all mankind.[4]

Since then, productivity motivation programs have become recognized as an effective leadership tool to counter lagging productivity. So says the Maritz Company of St. Louis. For over fifty years, Maritz has been in the business of helping their clients motivate people with what they call "Psychic Income"—income from honor and recognition. Maritz provides their clients with the symbols of success through merchandise and travel. Behavior is goal-directed, and when followers recognize an attractive goal, they are more prone to perform better and faster. Yet, in comparison to a tangible reward, say a watch, the recognition or honor from leaders and other followers is many times more important.

More organizations are structuring their pay so that workers get adequate basic pay, additional rewards for increases in personal competence, and special incentive pay or bonuses based on the performance of the individual or small groups. More and more of the special bonuses are coming monthly or quarterly.

Successful incentive programs require clear goals, good feedback, and accurate measurement. Nearly all tasks can be tailored to fit these criteria. Merchandise, travel, and recognition awards seem to have more lasting impact because they bring to mind pleasant images and fantasies. Money, on the other hand, tends to be rather cold and unemotional.

By applying Skinner's ideas, Emery Air Freight claims it saved $650,000 in one year. To increase productivity, Emery (1) specified the desired behavior (set the standards), (2) required the employee to provide continuous feedback (keep daily records), and (3) provided positive reinforcers (recognition, and so on) when production improved.[5]

Poor performance and declining production are major problems in today's organizations. Performance is surely guided by rules, regulations, structure, discipline, standards, and policies. However, research in the behavioral sciences has proven that punitive and negative measures do not increase productivity. This may be the most difficult lesson for leaders to learn from the Power Management Concept. Unfortunately, we are cued by the problems caused by followers. When mistakes are made, we can immediately recognize the damage it does to the organization. Many times leaders feel that a punitive verbal attack on the follower will cure the problem. While it may seem to relieve the immediate problem, the long-range effect of the attack will reduce the influence of the leader.

On the other hand, we are not cued by the productive performance of followers. We must learn to recognize and show appreciation for good performance. Again this is a difficult lesson, but it is just as true for our followers as it is for children.

MOTIVATION AND THE POWER MANAGEMENT MODEL

Many leaders have been disappointed in trying to use motivational techniques in a real situation. They find that what they have been taught in a course or read in a book is not effective. Their attitude then becomes one of "I have tried that, and it doesn't work."

Too often training in motivation is general in nature where the leader is told that certain techniques will be universally effective. The assumption is that all incentives will work for all followers. This is not true. For example, giving more responsibility for an activity may be motivating for one follower but not for another.

While it is fair to say that there is such a thing as group motivation, it is also true the group must meet the individual needs of the members much like the Super Bowl team that is motivated by team spirit but also gives each member of the team personal incentives for playing hard.

Like the Super Bowl team, an organization is made up of individuals with differing personalities and levels of needs. Even within the same person, motives change in relationship to the circumstances. A follower may feel very comfortable performing certain tasks and very insecure doing others. The motivation for the two situations will be quite different.

Even though people today are freer to do things for their own reasons, leaders must explore methods of providing a variety of incentives which meet individual needs in the organization. What we want to do as leaders is to increase the probability that an incentive will work. By using the Power Management leadership model, we can use the best fit motivator under the circumstances. See Figure 9-1.

FIGURE 9-1.   Motivation by Quadrant.

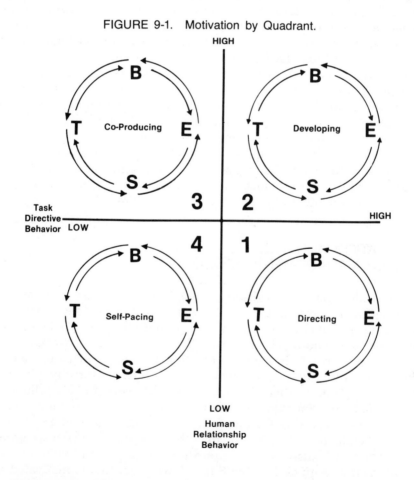

Quadrant One calls for the leader to use the directive leadership behavior. Again, this assumes that all of the power elements indicate closer supervision of the task. The directive leadership style implies that there are circumstances (power elements) that are unstable and more of the leader's attention is needed. However, the directive style does not imply a coercive type of behavior. Leaders interested in motivating followers in Quadrant One (directing) should:

- Eliminate unnecessary threats or yelling because such activities create more insecurity and less motivation.
- Make sure that followers understand what is expected. When followers are told what to do and when, where, and how to do a task, they feel more secure in the task assignments. Security, more often than not, is motivating to inexperienced followers.
- While the task at this level may at times be boring, the leader should make sure the results of good performance are rewarded.
- Reinforce and reward an individual for following directions. The reinforcement tends to serve as a motivation for the follower to be careful and listen to directions in the future.
- Focus on the individual's performance when giving feedback and not the individual. When there are performance problems, the leader should attempt to minimize the emotional conflict that may result between leader and follower. When we attack an individual, it is demotivating and becomes an emotional problem.

In Quadrant Two (developing), the leader should strive to motivate followers by:

- Giving followers the reasons behind the task assignment. This helps them understand the task and, in addition, allows the leader to communicate more closely with followers.
- Helping followers see the significance and relevance of what they are doing. Followers feel more motivation to accomplish a task when they know the significance of it to them and the organization. Much time is wasted by followers if they do not see the urgency or relevance of task assignments.
- Showing and communicating confidence in the follower when performance improves. Motivation is enhanced when followers are recognized for their developing skills.
- Developing an interest in the work that each follower is doing.

Leaders using the Quadrant Three (coproducing) style of leadership should motivate followers by:

- Starting to minimize the use of organization power with the follower because the motivating influence becomes one of involvement and cooperation, not rules.

- Recognizing the follower's contribution to the solutions of organizational problems.
- Letting the follower participate in making decisions that affect him or her.
- Letting the follower feel a sense of power or control over his or her own situation in the organization.
- Asking the follower to express his or her own opinion without fear of retribution. At this point, the leader can afford and should welcome this two-way communication.

In the Quadrant Four (self-pacing) leadership style, the leader should:

- Provide the follower with some flexibility and choice in how to accomplish the task. The motivating effect is that the follower feels more independent to use his or her own judgment.
- Give the appropriate responsibility to the follower to carry out the task assignment.
- Provide the follower with a feeling of trust and support.
- Encourage the follower to set his or her own goals.
- Let the follower engage in challenging and novel activities which stimulate his or her own creativity. Remember that this type of motivation is most appropriate in Q4 because the follower has the power elements and can be trusted to make effective judgments.

We can see that there is a time and place to use specific motivational tools. In fact, using the incorrect incentive can be counterproductive. For example, it may be demotivating to ask a person belonging in Q1 to take the responsibility for a task when the circumstances of the power elements are poor. Responsibility in that case is not a motivation. In other words, a motive in one case is not a motive in another.

PERSONALITY TYPES AND MOTIVATION

When using motivational tools, we must also take individual personality types into account. What is an incentive to one type of personality may not be to another. Considering personality type helps further personalize the motivation process. The following is a description of motivators that can be used with the different personality types.

Bold Personality

- Since the High B is stimulated by power, give him or her some authority as soon as possible.
- The Bold personality likes to work independently on a task, so provide that opportunity as an incentive.
- The Bold individual is motivated by a challenging task. However, clear instructions must be given before the Bold starts the task.
- Since the High B works well in a variety of situations, changing tasks is often motivating.
- The Bold personality likes work that is active and should be given the opportunity to move around.

Expressive Personality

- Since the High E likes to be around other people, give him or her a chance to work on team activities or tasks.
- The High E is usually a good communicator and is stimulated by using his or her persuasive skills.
- Let the High E have the opportunity to motivate others by personal or group interaction.

Sympathetic Personality

- The sympathetic personality is motivated by having a stable environment, so the leader needs to reassure the High S more often than he or she does other personality types.
- The High S also is stimulated by having a set schedule with little variation.
- The High S needs to be shown appreciation for task accomplishment—often.
- Since the High S is not motivated by constant change, he or she will be better motivated when given time to adjust to new procedures.

Technical Personality

- The Technical type personality responds to order in the environment. Rules and standards make for a more productive performance.
- The leader should reduce the risk of any task assignment by providing organization to the work.
- When assigned a new task, the High T will require more detailed explanations about where, when, and how to do the task.

Analyzing how to motivate different personality types is very important. The presence of risk and challenge is stimulating to the High B and demotivating to the High T. The leader's task, in motivating others, is to provide incentives that cause the follower to work for, not against, organizational goals. Only when personality is recognized as a factor in motivation will the leader be successful.

VALUES AS MOTIVATORS

Values are based on our ideas of how to achieve power. Positive power values include truth, love, justice, order, freedom, fairness, kindness, and so on. On the other hand, negative power values include prejudice, hate, bondage, injustice, anarchy, and brutality. However, human beings can be motivated to gain power by either positive or negative ways. In other words, one person may feel that by telling the truth a positive power position will be achieved with another individual. On the other hand, some people may feel the only way to overcome their weakness and thus gain power over another is through intimidation or brutality.

Demotivation is caused by the loss of power and feelings of inferiority. Individuals can become passive or aggressive because of the loss of power. This is particularly true with prolonged powerlessness. Values are sometimes violated by a person trying to overcome the sense of inferiority. The incentives to succeed can be either good or bad. For instance, one person may try to overcome a sense of powerlessness by showing kindness to others while another may resort to brutality.

It is also true that negative values are those that tend to enslave us. Yet there is no guarantee that internal negative incentives will be any less enslaving than negative external incentives. In other words, a follower can feel helpless because of the actions of a leader or he or she can cause his or her own situation to be less powerful. For example, when a follower steals from a leader and is caught, it results in a less powerful position for the follower. In more subtle ways, followers can reduce their own power by making power plays in the organization.

FOLLOWER MOTIVATION
AND ORGANIZATIONAL OBJECTIVES

It is the leader's task to direct followers in the accomplishment of organizational objectives. The follower must be willing to submit to certain controls that increase performance. Submission, however, is not the same as inferiority. To yield oneself to the power of another for mutual benefit is at the heart of the leader/follower relationship. It is the perception of mutual benefit that motivates the follower to accomplish organizational goals. Followers whose needs are being met will work more productively than when personal needs are not being met. A follower's motivation to work toward organizational goals is the result of positive external and internal incentives facilitated by the leader and the organization. It is doubtful that many good leaders can motivate followers to work for poor organizations and vice versa.

The leaders of any organization must plan a close and precise path for the motivation of followers (see Figure 9-2). The three vital steps necessary for this are:

1. Identify organizational objectives in very specific terms. These objectives include product, profit, service, growth, and so on.

2. Identify the kinds of follower behavior needed to accomplish the objectives. These behaviors may include time management, product quality maintenance, good interpersonal relations, positive customer relations, and others.

3. Select and administer incentives that reward followers for the behavior identified in Step 2. These incentives take the form of both social and material rewards. And, as discussed earlier, leaders must be careful to match incentives with the specific quadrant and personality characteristics of the follower.

FIGURE 9-2. Motivation Path.

| Identify Organizational Objectives | → | Identify Supportive Follower Behaviors | → | Select and Administer Incentives |

The idea, of course, is to bring the follower's behavior as close as possible to the behavior needed to accomplish the task. When followers see the positive results of this behavior for them individually, they will be motivated to achieve organizational goals. It is difficult, however, for some followers to see the immediate rewards of doing a specific task. This is why it is important for the leader to continuously communicate organization and task goals. In fact, most followers will respond more to the immediate rewards of doing a specific task if they are meaningful and the leader provides them systematically.

Again, the most useful motivational tools for the leader are those which move followers up their own power cycle from powerlessness to powerful, from an inferior position to a superior position, and from unsuccessful activities to successful activities. This transition up the power cycle for a follower is toward the positive use of his or her own power with beneficial outcomes for the organization.

Many times it is up to the leader to create reasonable expectations in the follower. Left to his or her own imagination, the follower's perspective of the rewards for doing a task may be distorted. Figure 9-3 shows how expectation and perception affect motivation.

FIGURE 9-3.   Behavior Strength.

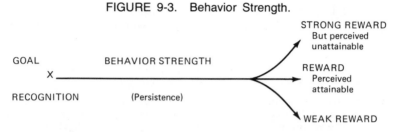

An individual recognizes that a reward is possible if he or she displays a certain type of behavior. The persistence of that behavior depends on the individual's perception of whether or not a reward is attainable and if it is worth the effort. For instance, if we were to recognize that we needed a new car, our behavior toward that end would depend on affordability, our current financial situation, and our general perception of the possibility. The type of car we buy is perceived to be attainable. It may be that an expensive sports car has great appeal but is unattainable, and not much energy is expended toward its purchase. On the other hand, neither would we use much energy to buy a nice but plain car if we see a more expensive car within our reach.

Again, the point is that leaders must help followers adjust their perceived attainable rewards. Even the most experienced followers do not make accurate judgments about objectives at times. Consequently, they settle for less quality and only adequate performance. The leader must hold high expectations for followers and communicate them in positive ways to followers.

POWER DISCIPLINE

How do leaders correct behavior that is unproductive? Certainly human beings behave in ways that do not contribute to the accomplishment of organizational goals. This entire book was written with the idea of helping leaders become effective at influencing the productive behavior of followers. The Leadership Language, Power Communication, Power Motivation, and the Power Management Model were all constructed to help leaders be more effective.

However, even after our best efforts as leaders, followers will make mistakes, use wrong procedures, and sometimes be immature in judgment. When everything we know about effective leadership fails, we must take some action to discipline the follower. Otherwise, the organizational goals will be compromised.

There are two discipline approaches being advocated in many leadership development programs with which we disagree. The first technique is discipline by showing anger and expressing disappointment in the follower. After this exchange, the leader then expresses confidence that the follower can do better. The second technique is to touch the follower on the arm or shoulder and softly and sincerely express concern about the unproductive behavior. Both of these extreme forms of discipline have no place in a mature and effective organization.

Much of the time the use of anger is like the old army saying "Ready, Fire, Aim." Anger is either misplaced or unproductive. Those who justify anger as a disciplinary tool do not talk about all of the other factors affecting poor performance, including the leader's behavior, before using anger. Moreover, research indicates that the show of anger to followers has diminishing returns.

Likewise, the use of touch with unproductive followers can be very dangerous. This is particularly true in business, education, and government. The leader who takes the chance of touching a follower also takes the chance of ending up in court. Touching, like the use of anger for discipline, can be interpreted too many ways to be used as a general technique.

What, then, can a leader do to discipline an unproductive follower who has been found to need it after analysis? The following procedures are suggested:

1. Talk to the follower in private as one adult to another about the performance problem.
2. Have the follower verbally commit to a specific change in behavior that will solve the performance problem.
3. Set a time for the problem to be corrected.
4. Describe the consequences if the problem is not solved.
5. Express concern about the performance problem but do not attack the follower personally.
6. Express confidence that the follower has the ability to solve the performance problem and that nothing else will do.

The Procedure above implies that all other communication and motivational tools have consistently been tried and nothing has worked. The procedure also implies that the leader and follower have come to some new understanding of the situation yet have maintained a working relationship.

Unfortunately, in these days of drug abuse, home problems, and alcoholism, the leader is sometimes faced with performance problems that neither he nor the follower can solve. It is realistic to think that the leader may need to find help in the community for these kinds of organizational problems. It is much better to help correct such problems and save a trusted follower than it is to start over again with a new employee.

PERSONAL FOLLOWER DEMOTIVATORS

Most of us are faced with internal conflicts and self-doubts from time to time. When someone does a better job than we do, we become self-conscious. Because of this constant comparison, we have self-doubts and are demotivated in certain situations when our status, prestige, and authority is reduced.

Several demotivating powers which are self-imposed can be identified:

1. Riskless power. This type of power keeps us from taking risks because it disturbs the order of events and because of the greater possibility of failure.

2. Traditional Power. When we want to do things the way they have always been done, we have been trapped by traditional power. This is a tendency to conform to past procedures even though there may be better ways of performing.

3. Clarity Power. This type of power occurs when we avoid the unknown or situations that lack clarity. This power demands that we know the future before going on.

4. Discomfort Power. When we perceive change to be painful or discomforting, we do not persist. We do not look at the long-range benefits because the short-term discomfort is too apparent.

5. Single Vision Power. Not seeing the several sides of an issue or not integrating ideas is single vision power. When we look at things only one way, it limits our personal creativity.

6. Nonappreciation Power. This is present when the individual does not evaluate his or her own strengths or the strengths of other people. This lack of appreciation of available resources hinders personal performance.

7. Nonaggressive Power. When we hesitate to express our ideas or stand up for our beliefs, we are troubled by nonaggressive power. The quality of our ideas may be good, but we do not like to push them on others.

Most of these personal follower demotivators can be overcome in time with the leader's help. When followers feel more secure, they begin to be motivated in more productive ways.

DEMOTIVATORS FROM LEADERS

Leadership at its worst can be called punk leadership. It is based on self-serving and self-protective motives. At least four types of punk leadership exist. They are as follows:

1. PYB Leadership. This type of leader uses the "Protect Your Behind" method of leadership and can be heard saying, "It's not my fault!" or "Who is responsible for this?"
2. Punt and Kick Leadership. This is leadership through the use of fear, intimidation, and ridicule. This leader believes the best method of leadership is through coercion.
3. Patch Things Up Leadership. In this leadership mode, the leader works on symptoms and not problems. He or she is satisfied to patch up the old system, ignore planning, and disregard the concerns of the follower.
4. Pacify Upper Leadership Leadership. This leader tells his or her leaders what they want to hear. The upper leaders do not get the truth or vital information upon which to make intelligent leadership decisions.

These four punk leadership methods all backfire in time. They are used because the leader is unsure of the job or has a feeling of powerlessness, or because it has always been done that way. It is easy to see how demotivating punk leadership would be to followers. Each of these leadership types decrease the power base of the follower and the leader, and no positive relationships are built. Eventually, the organizational system will break down.

THE LEADER AS A MODEL

Leaders who provide good role models can expect higher performance from followers. The leader, in essence, becomes a teacher by actions, not words. The positive personal behavior of leaders will exert a greater influence on followers than the behavior of inconsistent and poorly organized leaders.

We have discussed at great length the fact that human beings are constantly comparing themselves to others. Styles, fashions, fads, and peer pressure are all the results of our comparing themselves to others. The expected behavior is dictated by the trend setter. This is true in leadership. The leader sets the trend for followers and also sets the expectations of behavior in the organization.

In summary, since individuals have different motives for behaving, the motivational tools which the leader uses must be tailored to each follower. By using the Power Management Model as a guide, the leader can identify effective motivators at each level of the follower's development. In addition, each personality type should be motivated in a different way.

Effective leaders use a variety of motivational tools in an organization. By studying people and how each type is motivated, the leader can build not only personal power but also an outstanding organization.

NOTES

1. Abraham H. Maslow, *Motivation and Personality* (New York, N.Y.: Harper and Row Publishers, 1954).
2. Frederick Herzberg, Bernard Mausner, and Barbara Snyderman, *The Motivation to Work* (New York, N.Y.: John Wiley and Sons, Inc., 1959).
3. B. F. Skinner, *Science and Human Behavior* (New York, N.Y.: The Macmillan Company, 1953).
4. James F. Lincoln, *Incentive Management* (Cleveland, Ohio: The Lincoln Electric Company), p. 129.
5. "At Emery Air Freight: Positive Reinforcement Boosts Performance," *Organizational Dynamics*, Vol. 1, No. 3 (Winter 1973), pp. 41-50.

Interpersonal Power Systems

From a physiological point of view, the human being is weak and would not last long if left alone in a primitive forest. Consequently, the human being, more than any other member of the animal kingdom, has banded together for self-preservation. The realization of the interdependence between people is the recognition of the essence of the human experience.

Because of this interdependence, the human species has developed highly sophisticated systems of interpersonal interactions. In this text, we will call them *interpersonal power systems*. The interaction that takes place between two people is characterized by a constant struggle for power—sometimes violent but most often very subtle. The interpersonal power systems that develop in a relationship can be fine and delicate, cunning and crafty, or elusive and tenuous.

This chapter will explore the interpersonal relationships in the leadership process. The management of power by the leader necessitates an understanding of the interpersonal power systems that evolve between individuals and how the positive use of interpersonal power systems can benefit all involved. These positive power systems should be developed between the leader and the follower, between the followers themselves, and between leaders.

TYPES OF INTERPERSONAL POWER SYSTEMS IN ORGANIZATIONS

Power systems that develop between individuals depend on the purpose of the relationship. For instance, the power system that evolves between followers is different from the leader-follower power system. The purpose of each of these relationships is for varying reasons. While the leader-follower relationship cannot be the same as the follower-follower, it can still be positive.

Although the leader may not be directly involved, he or she needs to be aware of the power systems between others in the organization. Any organization is affected by the interpersonal relations of each of the followers because the performance of tasks by followers will be determined by negative and positive interpersonal power systems. What follows is a brief examination of each of the types of interpersonal power systems found in an organization. For instance, when two people have a great deal of antagonism toward each other, teamwork is hindered if not impossible. The negative relationship may develop to the point where neither party can function. On the other hand, when a relationship is positive, teamwork is enhanced and performance should be high.

Leader-Follower Power Systems

The two major concerns in the leader-follower power system are the goals or tasks and the human relationships. The leader attempts to influence the behavior of the follower toward a preconceived goal. If this attempt fails, no leadership has taken place. While the leader may make another attempt, the power to influence has been weakened. The power system has less reason for survival. Let us say, for example, the parent wants the child to make up his or her bed and says so to the child. If there is no positive power system between the two, the leadership attempt is apt to fail.

As mentioned earlier, the reason positive interpersonal power systems develop is because of mutual benefit. This is true in the leader-follower relationship. The mutual benefit concept can be positive or negative. For example, when a leader refrains from causing the follower pain and the follower performs the task because of it, the follower benefits. The follower's performance was obtained by negative means—no pain inflicted by the leader. When the positive mutual benefit concept is used, the submission of the follower's energy, time, and talent to the task is not an inferior position in the power system. However, there are many implied benefits to the follower that are never communicated by the leader. Only recently has there been an effort to train leaders in the conscious and planned rewarding of the follower's productive behavior.

The three positions in the leader-follower relationship are these:

Position 1.	The leader imposes his or her wishes on the follower who sees no personal benefit from doing the task.
Position 2.	The follower refuses to do the task for the leader because the positive benefits of not doing it outweigh the negative results.
Position 3.	The follower performs the task because he or she is aware of the overall positive benefits.

In the economics of leadership, the leader expects to get something in return for engaging the follower. Yet the same can be said for the follower. It is a simplistic idea to say that a follower or leader will yield something and not expect something in return. Again, lasting relationships are based on mutual benefit.

Leader-Leader Power Systems

Interpersonal power systems develop between leaders. Coalitions between leaders of equal power positions form within the organization. However, this type of coalition evolves only when the two leaders perceive themselves as equals. Otherwise, an informal leader-follower relationship may become active. For instance, leaders of equal rank on an organizational chart may not perceive themselves that way. One may exert influence over the other without a formal structure. This may happen when there is a new leader in the formal structure without much experience. The new leader feels uncomfortable in the new role and asks the more experienced leader for help.

Because each human being is constantly comparing himself or herself to others, the equal power system between leaders becomes difficult. Leaders see themselves in competition with other leaders, and the desire to move from a perceived inferior position to a superior one is human nature. There are two positions in the interpersonal power system between leaders:

Position 1.	The two leaders are in a competitive mode and vie for resources, personnel, information, and so on in

order to outperform other leaders in the organization.

Position 2.   The two leaders form a coalition in order to develop mutual benefits for their organizations or units. Both attempt to move from a position of weakness to a more favorable power arrangement in the organization.

The leader/leader power system is influenced by the personal and position powers of each and, consequently, takes on a more unstable atmosphere. The question becomes one of "How much depth should this interpersonal power system have?" or "How much trust can I place in the other leader?" The new leader is in this position. The experienced leader may see an opportunity to undercut the competition and give the new leader bad advice. Unless both see mutual benefit in the relationship, the power system will be tenuous at best.

Follower-Follower Power Systems

Interpersonal power systems between followers of equal position power are freer from the pressures of competition. There is more loyalty to the relationship, and the power system becomes a place to vent frustrations. The relationship involves one of emotional as well as social support.

Follower-follower power systems tend to be a protective shield from the problems of the organization. An individual's self-concept is more a product of this relationship than any other. The idea of "divided we fall" is operating here, and the two parties in the system can persist with a behavior or belief much longer as a team than they can acting alone. It is likely that if one member of the follower system is rebuked by the boss, the other follower will provide emotional support and, in some cases, truth is denied. That is, the boss is wrong and the followers are right even in the face of contrary evidence.

The two positions of the follower-follower interpersonal power system are as follows:

Position 1.   The two followers see no perceived mutual benefit in developing a power system. Each party may feel secure in other relationships in the organization or have a perceived difference in values, background, style, and so on with the other followers.

Position 2.   The two followers see mutual benefit in forming an interpersonal power system for various reasons. Pure friendship is rarely a reason for a follower-follower power system in an organization. Most often the relationship forms for self-protection against the internal pressures of the organization. Leaders may be the cause of some of the pressures and working conditions may influence some additional concerns.

The follower-follower interpersonal power system can be very stable. The degree of stability is determined by the mutual benefits of the relationship.

In summary, the mutually beneficial interpersonal power system is like a savings account; deposits are made, draw interest, and are withdrawn when needed. In other words, the other person becomes a resource of support for building our own power base. In return, we support the building of their power base.

Positive interpersonal power systems are developed for mutual benefit. In fact, it is a painful experience to dismantle a positive interpersonal power system. Each party may feel a loss of power because of the removal of the emotional and social support.

The development of groups in an organization, however, is much more complex although the members are motivated by mutual benefits. Group dynamics in the organization and the emergence of informal leaders in groups is an interesting subject within itself. While space does not permit a full discussion of this concept, group behavior depends on the circumstances, the personalities involved, and the benefits to its members.

FOLLOWER MATURITY

One of the concerns for the leader in an organization is the maturity of the follower. Immaturity affects task performance as well as interpersonal relations within the organization. Immaturity is almost always rewarded with rule-centered leadership. For instance, if a person damages a piece of equipment because he or she did not read the directions, this would be an immature act. The leader will set rules for the use and operation of the equipment. Rules are necessary because of the possible immature behavior of one person.

However, there are different types of immaturity. In addition, there is as much deviation of immaturity within one person as there is between two people. Immaturity, then, depends on the specific activity or emotional context of a given situation. For instance, a person may be able to perform a task but is emotionally immature around certain people. This emotional immaturity affects the follower's performance. A person may, for example, be a fine singer but lack the maturity to perform in public.

It may be that the best test of the emotional maturity for an individual is to look at his or her goal-directed behavior. The more self-serving the goal, the more immature the individual. How does the leader know the maturity level of the follower? How can the leader develop the emotional and task-related maturity of the follower?

First, we must identify the individual's stage of maturity. Secondly, we should determine the emotional and task maturity of the person. Notice in Figure 10-1 that we are discussing the maturity

FIGURE 10-1.   The Power Cycle and Maturity.

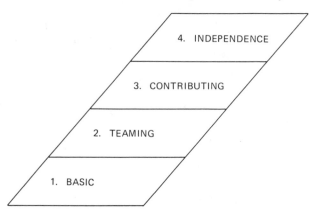

of the leader *and* follower. In trying to find the level of maturity, we can identify four stages of development:

1. **Basic Maturity.** A person in the basic maturity stage is learning how, when, and where to do things. This individual is being cared for and directed by others. This is an immature position and the person's power base is inferior when compared to others.

2. **Teaming Maturity.** An individual at this stage is learning the reasons for doing things certain ways. At this stage, the person develops a wide range of communication skills and how to be part of a team in group and community living. The skills of working for and with others are practiced at this stage.

3. **Contributing Maturity.** Because the person is now ready to have the responsibility for decisions, he or she must learn to test those decisions in the real world. At this level, the indi-

vidual can make a contribution to the organization through a high degree of participation. Again, however, the testing of those ideas is very important in the maturity process.

4. **Independence Maturity.** Full maturity is when an individual can make responsible decisions for himself or herself and others. There is an increase in the use of interpersonal skills because leading and influencing others becomes more probable. Maturity at this level means that the individual can self-pace his or her own behavior and that behavior tends to be for the good of the organization and even for humanity.

Maturity is not stationary even though general maturity is perceived as somewhat stable. The maturity level is a function of the circumstances. For example, an eighty-year-old person flying on an airplane for the first time can be very immature in that situation.

When we increase our personal power base, we increase our maturity. The power cycle previously discussed gives us insight into an individual's maturity based on his or her stage in the power cycle. In other words, the individual's power base stage and maturity level are the same. For example, if the follower's level in the power cycle is in the first level (Basic), we can be relatively sure that his or her maturity will be at that level. When an individual is at the lower level of the power cycle, the need to know how, when, what, and so on is not only a function of ability but also of maturity. Followers will feel more secure and be able to develop if close supervision is provided at this level.

How we perceive ourselves in a given situation dictates our level of maturity behavior. For example, the interaction between two people inevitably includes comparison. When we do a better job than the other person, we feel more mature and successful. The problem is that in reality the performance of both may be poor. Feelings of success may create a false sense of maturity. This is why the leader needs to maintain an objective level of expectation for followers.

This is a problem in interpersonal relations for the leader. Standards of performance should not be based on the highest maturity level of a given follower but should be developed around proven standards. In other words, standards of performance and expectations for the quality of work should be higher than the average maturity level of the followers. The leader must communicate this expectation and at the same time maintain a mutually beneficial power system.

DEALING WITH
NEGATIVE POWER DEVIATIONS

Again, the leader must have a way to analyze the problems that take place between members of the organization. This, of course, is the first step to solving interpersonal and organizational problems. When we can determine in a simple and understandable way what interpersonal problems exist or may exist, we can prevent the conflict. Using the Negative Power Deviation (NPD) analysis is easy and helps to reduce the emotional conflict when the leader needs to make a decision about the follower's performance.

The following examples of NPD between the leader and the follower will help us better understand how to analyze the interaction process. Consider this dialogue:

LEADER: Mason, get in here. You stupid incompetent! You know I'm going to New York tomorrow. Why didn't you make hotel and plane reservations? What do I pay you for? Are you so stupid you can't take some initiative? Think, man, think! I'm not going to spend my day telling you every little thing to do. And look at this, you ordered 20 cases of product supply! When did I OK 20 cases? Huh? You'd better be careful, understand? Now, get back to work.

FOLLOWER: (Leaves the room and speaks to the secretary.) You just can't please that Hunter. Nothing I do is right. If I take initiative, I'm told I'm overstepping my bounds. If I don't, I'm incompetent.

It is obvious that there is interpersonal conflict between the two. The leader is being highly directive (Q1 Style) and is even using that style inappropriately. The follower feels that he or she should be in Q3 where initiative is usually approved by the leader. If the leader is using Q1 leader behavior and the follower feels he should be in Q3, there is a −2 negative power deviation (−2 NPD).

If the leader in this instance is interested in higher production from Mason, he must move out of the Q1 leadership behavior to a higher and more appropriate level. Remember, the idea is to preserve both the leader's and follower's power bases.

Sometimes the leader's behavior is inconsistent and confuses the follower. Consider the interaction in this scene.

FOLLOWER: Mr. Hunter, I've been here four months now. Give me some feedback on how I'm doing. Do you have any complaints or compliments?

LEADER: Yes, Jean, you're doing a fine job. Your work is very good. You've carried out assignments competently. You're doing a fine job for us.

FOLLOWER: Good. In that case, do you remember when I first started to work here—you promised me a $100-a-month raise after three months. Well, I've been here for four months and if you have no complaints, I'd like to have that raise.

LEADER: *(Mr. Hunter pulls back from his desk and looks at his finger-nails.)* Jean, I've decided that instead of giving you a $100-a-month raise now, I'll be able to give you a $150 raise after your sixth month here. That would give you an extra $100 for the year. And, when you came in, you asked if I had any complaints. Well, I have noticed you are sometimes late coming back from lunch breaks and you don't always seem to have the daily reports ready when I get here in the mornings. Watch these things.

FOLLOWER: Yes, sir. But, if overall you're pleased . . .

LEADER: I am; that's why I'm going to work out this better deal for you than a small raise now. That extra $100 on the year is only the start that you'll get from compounding the difference in $100 a month more now versus $150 a month extra in just two more months. You'll be better off—just trust me. OK? (Walking Jean out the door.)

FOLLOWER: Well, OK. (Looks puzzled)

What was the leadership behavior at the end of the scene? How did it change from the first behavior in the scene? What quadrant was the follower in? This scene is interesting because the behavior of the leader changed during the interaction.

At first, the leader said that Jean was doing a fine job and there is some indication that both the follower and leader were even in Q4. However, when the follower asked for the promised raise, the leader's behavior slipped back into a Q2 leadership behavior style which is an NPD of -2.

In this case, the leader is inconsistent in his leadership behavior and also moves out of the correct quadrant in the treatment of the follower. If the leader is interested in the continued high productivity of the follower, consistent behavior is necessary.

The consequences of continuous NPDs are the erosion of the leader's power base with a follower. When the leader does not take the time to use personal power with a follower, something like the following may happen:

LEADER: I need this typed today.

FOLLOWER: I'll see what I can do but we're two days behind with our regular work, and that looks like it would take two girls working most of the afternoon.

LEADER: This is a priority item. Don't you do priority over regular typing?

FOLLOWER: Yes, but one of our girls is out sick.

LEADER: Well, surely you have someone who is working today.

FOLLOWER: Yes, but their work has already been assigned to them today.

LEADER: Well, can't you reassign it?

FOLLOWER: Yes, but they've already started on it.

LEADER: Look this must be done today. If it is not finished by 5:00, I'll go to the boss. How you do it is your business. Just do it.

It is obvious that the follower (in Q3) felt little motivation to help the leader (in Q1). The leader was not a source of positive reinforcement for the follower, and the situation went from bad to worse. Productivity suffered for both the follower and leader. The leader was under a time pressure to get the assignment done and the only way out seemed to be intimidation.

There was an NPD of −3 in this case, which resulted in anger, frustration, and little production. Had the leader established early a positive power system with the follower, the chance of priority reassignment would have been greater.

The leader needs to be aware of NPDs between other members in the organization. The next case points out how NPDs can cause conflicts.

JACK: Excellent, Tom. That was a very thorough, insightful report. A very commendable job. I think we can pass this along to the Board without revision. What do you think? (Looking at the others gathered around the table.)

ADAM: I agree. Good job, Tom.

JEAN: Tom, I think you've covered all the bases. I can't think of anything to add.

BART: Well, I have a few comments. In the first place, there are a number of typographical errors and a number of grammatical errors. Just look here on page 86, for example. You've used the wrong form for the subject of a gerund. And on page 38, you've used the present tense when you should have used future perfect. We can't overlook these kind of errors. Also, gentlemen, this report is printed on cheap paper. Wouldn't look good for a report cleared by our committee to go out looking like this.

Jack, Adam, and Jean were all in Q4 as it related to the specific task of Tom's report. Bart's reaction, however, seems to be in Q1 which is a −3 NPD. In other words, negative power deviations can happen between followers and in groups. We also must remember that personality types play a part in NPDs at times. In this case study, Bart's personality was a High T and he was somewhat of a perfectionist in his approach to a task. This quality does not need to be diminished because it is useful, but Bart's communication style needs some adjustment. The leader can help mold an effective team if all of the team members know and understand how to communicate with other personality types.

In the next case, we will consider a zero NPD scene. We

should be able to recognize the quadrant and the personalities involved.

ERIC: Susan, it's great to have you with us. And I do want to introduce you to everyone, but I've got a crisis. I need 20 copies of this report in 30 minutes. Can you help?

SUSAN: OK. The copier is in which room?

ERIC: It's down the hall, third door on the left. It's a Royal copier. Have you used one before?

SUSAN: Not that brand.

ERIC: Well, let me get you started.

ERIC: Ah, here we are. Here are the instructions. And, you'll need legal-size paper. It's in this tray. Let me show you how to insert it into the machine.

SUSAN: OK. I've got that. And I just put the document here, select the number of copies, and start it.

ERIC: Right, and for the colored sheets, press this button; otherwise, the copies will be too dark.

SUSAN: OK. I can handle it.

Eric and Susan both have High B personalities. They both want quick results and use the direct communication style. Eric is in the directive leadership mode and Susan responds because the situation is new for her. Eric takes the time to show Susan how to use the new equipment, a step that will save time later. There is no NPD and both power bases are enhanced. And there is a comfortable interpersonal relationship between the leader and follower for this specific task.

Sometimes an NPD is the result of the leader not taking into account the personality of the follower. The follower may have all the power elements to complete the task but the communication style used by the leader is inappropriate. Consider this case.

ADAM: It's review time again.

BART: Sure is . . . seems to come around quicker every year.

ADAM: Well, this year I want you to take responsibility for departments 22 through 42.

BART: Me?

ADAM: Yes. I've come to respect the quality of your work, especially the attention to detail.

BART: Thanks. What do I do?

ADAM: Just move ahead on it. It's due in two weeks.

BART: Two weeks!

ADAM: Yes.

BART: Two weeks! That's impossible. I can't do it. Where do I start? What's the schedule? Come on, I need help.

ADAM: Calm down. It's nothing you can't handle. There's nothing new in this. When you run into specific problems, bring them to me. I'll help you keep everything on the level.

BART: But what's expected of me in the review? Sure, I've been on the other end, but never surveying other people's work. Is there a checklist? Who do I see? Have you got a timetable worked out?

Had Bart been given more details of how, when, where, and why, he may have felt more comfortable with the assignment. Bart is obviously a High T and likes structure, organization, and direction. As described, the interaction resulted in a −2 NPD. The leader, Adam, was in Q3 and Bart, the follower, felt that he needed to be in Q1. If the leader had been interested in the continued high quality of Bart's performance, he would have taken more time to prepare Bart for the task assignment.

Again, the use of the concept of NPDs is to reduce leader-follower conflicts to a simple and understandable form. Once we can analyze what is happening and how serious it is, we can make more productive problem-solving decisions.

POWER SYSTEMS
AND PERSONALITY TYPES

In the last case presented, it was pointed out that the personality type of the follower was one cause of the poor interpersonal relationship that developed. As we have discussed many times in this text, personality type must be considered by the leader in making task assignments. By understanding the interpersonal results of personality type interaction, the leader has an opportunity to form and be a part of highly productive activities in the organization. If, however, the leader ignores personality, personal conflicts are going to take away from productivity. There are two helpful things the leader can do.

First, the leader must recognize the potential for interpersonal conflict that may arise simply based on personality types. For instance, there is the potential for a great deal of natural conflict between a High B and a High T. The High B wants quick results and the High T wants to follow established procedures. This can lead to a negative power struggle between the two.

Secondly, if the leader knows the personality type of the followers, he or she can help followers understand how to work together in very productive ways. The High B can develop new ways of doing things and the High T can make sure that quality is maintained. The leader has turned a potential weakness into a plus because of the understanding of personality types.

Figure 10-2 shows the conflict potential in an organization

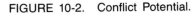

FIGURE 10-2. Conflict Potential.

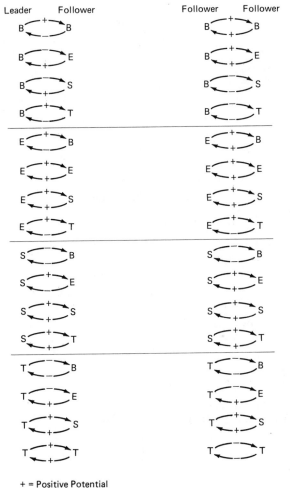

+ = Positive Potential
— = Negative Potential

between leaders and followers, and between followers and followers because of personality types. However, this figure is only an example of the potential for conflict and it should be understood that many constructive relationships develop among all personality types. It should be noted again that it is in the work situation that the conflict potential exists.

PERCEPTION, PERSONALITY, AND LEADERSHIP

While we have just discussed personality types and leadership, a word of caution needs to be added. The perception we have of others may not be consistent with their own self-perception. Most of us are unaware of how we are perceived by others. We all wear masks that protect our feelings. For instance, with the power of leadership comes the feeling of powerlessness because to lead is to invite risk. The leader feels powerless to control the outcome of risking. While a leader may try to project extreme rigidity, it is most likely that he or she is trying to control a situation in which he or she feels powerless.

In addition, the leader is faced with another perception dilemma. On the one hand, the leader is faced with becoming too familiar with followers and on the other, completely alienating them. The leader must walk the fine line between the two. In order to walk that fine line, the leader must be aware of his or her own personality style. There is a danger of the leader being perceived as too picky, too hard, too soft, or too carefree, just because of personality type. This is not to say that each of these types is not useful at times, but it really depends on the circumstances. The leader must work toward making perception and reality closer.

POSITIVE POWER SYSTEMS

The struggle for power is the beginning of creativity. When the leader and follower both gain power creativity, the organization is enhanced. Followers and leaders feel positive about their interpersonal power systems and in the struggle for positive power experience growth.

The forces that mold the interaction between two people are intelligence, maturity, personality, talent, and ability. These forces should be molded by the leader into working teams. Just as the power elements determine the power position of the leader in the organization, the same power elements affect interpersonal relations.

In building positive interpersonal power systems, the leader should

1. identify the purpose of the relationship,
2. provide mutual benefits for each party based on the purpose,
3. avoid negative power deviation by planning task assignments,
4. recognize follower maturity,

5. approach the follower with a task assignment with maturity, personality, and position elements in mind, and

6. above all, help followers gain personal power for themselves in the organization.

As we have pointed out many times, we are all interdependent. However, the most productive relationships develop when both parties benefit and a positive power system is allowed to grow. Leaders above all need this understanding. The use of the collective power of followers and leaders is the most productive way of achieving organizational goals. As a result of understanding the concept of Negative Power Deviation, we can analyze and prevent interpersonal problems. In addition, we should realize how personality affects performance when the teaming of followers is used. Moreover, the knowledge of how maturity relates to performance and the power cycle should be very helpful in developing followers.

11
Epilogue

A NEW LEADERSHIP STRATEGY
FOR AMERICA

Leaders in America need to regain their sense of direction. One reason it was lost was that the role of the leader became very complex. Each decision had more than one side, and leaders began to withdraw into less productive and more comfortable management roles. Leadership and its resulting use of power was downplayed. In fact, it was condemned.

In large measure, the obstacles that had always stimulated American ingenuity became roadblocks. Because there were no easy answers, leadership withdrew and energy dissipated. Few examples of strong and forceful leaders could be found.

It is time for the redefining of power and leadership in this country. Neither is negative unless good people allow them to be. Effective leadership and the positive use of power can be of immense benefit to mankind. However, effective leadership will start with each individual when the serious study of power and leadership take on new meaning.

We also need an American leadership system that reflects the diversity of backgrounds, circumstances, and personalities found in this country. Rather than the system calling for one best way of leadership or one answer to a performance problem, the new American system must provide the leader with a variety of tools to use in many environments and under many circumstances.

POWER IN ORGANIZATIONS

Power in today's organizations has moved from coercion to persuasion, from brainwashing to education, and from regimentation to participation. Yet there are only certain times when an organization can afford to be all democratic. By the same token, there are only certain times that an organization can afford to be autocratic. The mode of leadership depends on the nature of the organization and the circumstances. That mode needs, however, to be based on rational analysis and a measured response for the demands for change.

While it is laudable and wise for leaders to work toward more follower participation, it must be planned and encouraged under the right circumstances. Otherwise, another good movement will fail because of the lack of proper implementation. Blake and Mouton point out, "As long as people are antagonistic toward the authority being exercised on them, or have ceased being involved to the point of becoming apathetic, any effort to change norms will not be effective. Problems that are centered on the faulty use of power and authority can be solved only when managers learn better ways to exercise that power and authority, ways that promote involvement and active participation rather than indifference."[1]

There are at least two reasons that formal participation methods fail. First, some followers do not respond because of their personality type. These followers are more comfortable in the subordinate role and do not like the decision-making process because they are loyal to the leader. For them to make or participate in management decisions is a tendency foreign to their personality.

Secondly, leaders who jump into group decision-making activities are asking for trouble. Followers must develop the necessary skills, understanding, and attitudes before any of the power equalization methods are used. The preparation and training of followers to participate is not just "nice" but vital.

The objective of leaders should be to build the position power bases of every follower in the organization. This is a growth process and takes an understanding of the developmental level of each individual and of how an organizational system should support that development.

The idea of the distribution of power within and throughout an organization to reduce the abuse of power is not new. This lesson was learned many years ago, and national leaders like George Washington recognized the need of many to participate in the power of government. His observation is appropriate to all organizations. He said:

> The spirit of encroachment tends to consolidate the powers of all the departments in one, and thus to create, whatever the form of government, a real despotism. A just estimate of that love of power, and proneness to abuse it, which predominates in the human heart, is sufficient to satisfy us of the truth of this position. The necessity of reciprocal checks in the exercise of political power, by dividing and distributing it into different depositaries, and constituting each the guardian of the public weal against invasions by the others, has been evinced by experiments ancient and modern; some of them in our country and under our own eyes.[2]

In addition to the distribution of power within an organization, leaders must consider the effects of change on followers and organizational performance. When followers become frustrated and fearful about change, power plays are a natural outgrowth. Leaders must try to reduce power plays by involving followers in decisions and power whenever possible.

At the same time, we must be realistic about politics in organizations, especially larger ones. Followers have many motivations to work within an organization, and personal wants and needs are certainly involved. It is up to the leader to channel those motivations into productive activities for the organization.

Finally, interdependency and dependency are not the same where power is concerned. There is always the potential for the abuse of power in a dependency relationship. Furthermore, in the modern organization, that dependency reduces the efficiency of power because of the drag on resources, continuous supervision, the loss of time, and so on. The wise leader in an organization always tries to move followers from individual dependency to an interdependent team.

POSITION POWER

The position power of a leader in an organization is based on many factors or power elements. The strength of the position depends on the environment, resources, time, information, and so on. Different leadership approaches will be necessary if power elements are weak or if they are strong. Using the same leadership style in all circumstances reduces the position power of the leader because the leader is simply not meeting organizational needs.

Position Analysis is a tool that gives the leader a perspective of the strengths and weaknesses in the organization. It is, after all, the task of the leader to overcome soft spots in an organization. In addition, the leader who uses the position analysis process has some firm basis upon which to determine how to lead and how much supervision is needed under a certain set of circumstances.

A leader's position power is increased in the organization with the information derived from the careful analysis of the organization. That information is used to make more intelligent and productive leadership decisions about events and people. Rational and objective decisions help leaders gain position power and become more effective leaders.

PERSONAL POWER

Early leadership theorists tried to discover common leadership personality traits. If only we could define the common elements of leadership, then supposedly, the successful leaders could incorporate those traits into their own lives. Like the scout who is supposed to be loyal, brave, reverent, clean, and courteous, the leader could take on those characteristics of effective leadership and achieve greater results. Unfortunately, even if an effective list of traits were developed and commonly agreed upon as important to leadership success, little value would be produced by this effort. Regardless of a person's dedication to a cause, basic personality will make a person unique and unable to perfectly mimic the prescribed leadership traits. Again, even the most dedicated scout fails to be perfectly loyal, thrifty, reverent, clean, or courteous.

Moreover, even if a training program could be devised that would allow leaders to incorporate specific traits into their behavior patterns, no universally valid leadership traits can be found. Research has proven that when circumstances or situations change, the effectiveness of leaders also changes. There is no one set of behavior traits that will produce optimum results in all situations. For instance, one of the most successful field generals during World War II was General George Patton. However, the behavior traits that served him well in combat situations were totally inappropriate for the diplomatic tasks required of an Allied commander. The same traits that brought him honor on the battlefield almost destroyed his career when the shooting was far away. For this reason, management theories based on leadership behavior clusters such as Blake and Mouton's Managerial Grid fail to answer the specific problems that managers face in the day-to-day operation of a business. One set of leadership behaviors cannot work with all the complexities of the ever-changing business environment.

A response to this obvious deficiency was made by contingency management or situational management approaches that noted that organizational change requires a change in management leadership style. Situationalism as represented by the Hersey-Blanchard Model of Situational Leadership, contends that the appropriate approach to management must correspond to the maturity of the subordinate. As an individual grows in maturity on a specific task, the manager's leadership style must change with that individual. The key factor that determines appropriate leadership behavior is the maturity level of the subordinate. Maturity relates to the willingness and ability of the individual to assume responsibilities. This approach discounts the role of personality in affecting what leaders may perceive as maturity. All followers displaying a given perceived level of maturity are to be treated in a prescribed manner. Once again, the personality factors of individual workers are ignored.

What if, however, personality style is more important than either the situation or specific leader behavior? What if the characteristics of a leader's personality and the characteristics of a subordinate's personality have more to do with success than the other factors? Would we not be missing out on comprehensive leadership development by ignoring personality?

We first respond to another individual based on that individual's personality and how well it relates to our own. Our perception of the other person gives order to our social environment. Over the years, we learn to identify strong and weak personality traits in other people. This is a subtle but extremely important process. Early in our relationship with another person, questions of power, ambition, credibility, confidence, dependability, and rationality are tentatively answered. We incorporate this perception into our relationship with the other person. Moreover, this is a process which cannot be divorced from our social or professional life.

Perhaps leadership theorists have ignored the issue of personality because it has been hard to appropriately define. Characteristics, styles, manners, traits, attitudes, and so on all mix together to form our way of describing another's personality. Since such factors have not been easy to quantify, they have not been appropriate for use by those building leadership models who wish to cloak their products with the appearance of being scientific and quantifiably proven.

Research is now beginning to tell us that personality style is based on measurable reasons and not just on environmental accidents. Personality may be defined in terms of dominant behavior patterns. These patterns may be brain-hemisphere controlled or otherwise controlled by some biosociologic factor. Regardless of the relative importance of environment versus genetic factors, instruments have been developed that show that four distinct styles of personality exist. These styles of behavior must certainly influence the leadership style that the person will exhibit as a leader.

Obviously, the personality dimension is too important to leave out. Leaders and prospective leaders need to know their dominant personality style and how it affects them and others. The old statement that one cannot effectively lead others without first understanding himself or herself remains true today. The issues raised by situationalism and the Managerial Grid obviously must be considered. Leadership behavior and the factors of environmental situations are certainly important. However, they may only be considered appropriately when seen in light of the personality styles of both managers and subordinates.

We must help leaders understand their personality characteristics, identify the characteristics of their subordinates, and understand how the two relate in determining the appropriate leadership role. We must help leaders recognize similarities and conflicts that may exist between their personalities, the styles of their subordinates, and the leadership role itself. The influence of personality in handling situational issues clearly must be considered. If the element of personality is ignored, then the analysis is incomplete and the leadership process is lacking an essential element required for success.

A leader's personal power is increased by this understanding. When a leader is able to treat followers in accordance with their personality type, the performance of the follower will improve. In addition, when leaders help followers understand themselves, personal conflicts will be reduced in the organization and productivity in teaming will increase.

ACTION POWER

The leader must see himself or herself in a power process or cycle that is always changing. By understanding this power cycle, the leader can gain personal power and help followers develop power. We all progress or struggle to move up the power cycle through the different levels of power. Those levels include the Basic, which is the lowest, through Teaming and Contributing up to, finally, Independence (Figure 11-1).

The Power Cycle can be seen when applied to a simple task

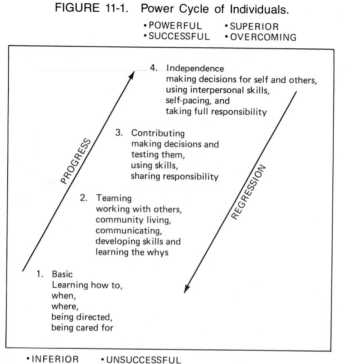

FIGURE 11-1. Power Cycle of Individuals.

- POWERFUL   - SUPERIOR
- SUCCESSFUL - OVERCOMING

4. Independence
   making decisions for self and others,
   using interpersonal skills,
   self-pacing, and
   taking full responsibility

3. Contributing
   making decisions and
   testing them,
   using skills,
   sharing responsibility

PROGRESS

REGRESSION

2. Teaming
   working with others,
   community living,
   communicating,
   developing skills and
   learning the whys

1. Basic
   Learning how to,
   when,
   where,
   being directed,
   being cared for

- INFERIOR   - UNSUCCESSFUL
- OVERCOME   - POWERLESS

which a follower is mastering or to the life process itself. If we understand that in all activity people struggle to move from positions of inferiority to superiority, we as leaders can help facilitate that movement in followers.

Consistent leadership will create a sense of trust among followers. However, the kind of consistency needed is based on the specific follower in a given circumstance. Changes in leadership styles without reason or wild changes in attitude and mood serve only to frustrate the best of followers. This type of behavior is called leapfrog leadership—leadership styles changing without reason. We should all remember that the characteristics of poor leadership include ineffectiveness, self-centeredness, oppressiveness, and inconsistency of behavior.

THE POWER MANAGEMENT MODEL

Because most of us cannot remember all of the complex factors involved in leadership, we need a model to serve as a tool for effective decision making. The Power Management Model described in this book represents the three major leadership areas which have been studied over the past 80 years. When the leader follows the three-step process in the model, decisions can be made with the assurance that the major factors of leadership have been considered (Figure 11-2).

FIGURE 11-2.   Power Management Model.

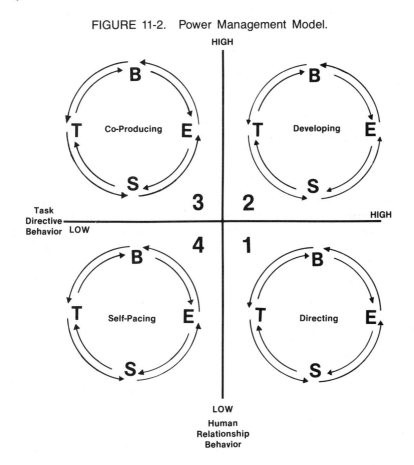

In addition, this book advocates a leadership language that uses unique symbols and terms to communicate leadership concepts. There are two reasons that the leadership language is important. First, it helps reduce the emotional conflict when leaders and followers talk about performance, and second, it simplifies the world of complex concepts that must be remembered by the leader into a common language. It is very similar to the idea of a computer language in that the leadership language saves time in making decisions.

Leaders who have no way of analyzing their own performance are prone to make the same mistakes over and over again. The Power Management Model helps leaders gain a frame of reference, a conceptual view, and a step-by-step process for making task assignments and other leadership decisions.

POWER COMMUNICATIONS

Productive communication is not easy. The leader must actively work at it and understand what is actually taking place when communicating. Moreover, we find two-way communication displacing one-way communication in the modern organization. Consequently, the art of communication for the leader becomes even more important.

We have discovered that the style of communications of the follower and leader has a great impact on how information is received. The personality type also influences how followers perceive leaders. This perception can be positive or negative. For instance, one characteristic of a punk leader is that he or she gives the outward impression of desiring two-way communication. In this case, the perception is false.

However, the wise leader will make a study of each follower's personality and communicate accordingly. Since it is known that each of the different personality types receives information in a unique way, the leader's communication effectiveness will depend on *how* he or she communicates with each. In addition, the power cycle level of the follower on a specific task gives us another way to plan our communications. The leader, for instance, under certain circumstances, uses the directing style of communications. And at other times, a leader will use the coproducing mode of communications.

The leader can develop personal power by improving communications skills. The effective transmission of information is the key to the performance of the organization. The leader must recognize that withheld information is just as powerful as information communicated. However, there are negative and positive sides to each.

Finally, we cannot deny that much of our communications is ego-centered. That is, information is power and we withhold or give it depending on how good it makes us feel. The clean, objective, unemotional, and unselfish use of communications is rare. All we can do as leaders is work toward that end.

POWER MOTIVATION

Like communications, the use of specific motivators depends on the power cycle level and personality of the follower. To a large degree, leaders must use specific motivators with followers because in the modern organization, coercive methods have been displaced with methods that appeal to the wants and needs of the individual. Finding the key, then, to motivating each follower to work for and support organizational goals is the key to higher productivity.

The Power Management concept is designed to help leaders see how specific motivators can be used depending on the circumstances and the follower's personality. By the same token, demotivators are discussed in this book which are either self-imposed or a result of punk leadership.

Just as in Position Analysis, the leader must analyze the circumstances and apply the proper motivators. The leader who does not systematically plan and use incentive rewards will be disappointed in the results. At the same time, the follower who works and serves an organization without reward and recognition is in a negative power system.

Organizations are, of course, made up of people who interact on an ongoing basis. Interpersonal relations depend upon the purpose of the interaction. Power systems are developed between individuals and can have various effects on productivity. The leader should understand these power systems and how they can be used to enhance organizational performance.

In addition, the leader needs to understand the maturity of followers and the level of development of the followers on the power cycle. Immaturity and power do not mix, yet followers must always be developing maturity enough to accept more power and responsibility. How this maturity is developed by the leader is described in this book.

It is also true that the leader needs a way to analyze and prevent emotional and personality conflicts within the organization. The interactions between people can be negative or create negative power deviations (NPD). The Power Management System of analyzing these deviations is important to the leader if increased productivity and greater harmony is desired.

In the modern organization, dependence has been displaced with interdependence. This means that more people work as teams and the ability to work together becomes critical. Since personality is involved in so much of the interpersonal conflict in an organization, the leader must understand how to reduce its negative effect and, in fact, how to use personality types to improve teamwork and perform-ance.

CONCLUSION

The best way for the use of negative power to continue is for good people not to use positive power. The responsibility of taking a lead-ership role cannot be taken lightly and must be studied as carefully as any other organizational concept. The effective leader continu-ously analyzes and plans leadership decisions. But more than that, the effective leader has an extra measure of commitment to serve self, the organization, and humanity. The charge to leaders is ex-pressed in this passage of Thomas Chalmers, the Scottish orator:

> Thousands of men breathe, move, and live; pass off the stage of life, and are heard of no more. Why? They did not a particle of good in the world; and none were blest by them, none could point to them as the instrument of their redemption; not a line they wrote, not a word they spoke, could be recalled, and so they perished—their light went out in darkness, and they were not remembered more than the insects of yesterday. Will you thus live and die, o man immortal? Live for something. Do good, and leave behind you a monument of virtue that the storms of time can never destroy. Write your name by kindness, love, and mercy, on the hearts of the thou-sands you come in contact with year by year, and you will never be forgotten. No, your name, your deeds, will be as legible on the hearts you leave behind as the stars on the brow of evening. Good deeds will shine as bright on the earth as the stars of heaven.[3]

NOTES

1. Robert R. Blake and Jane Srygley Mouton, *Productivity: The Human Side* (New York, NY: AMACOM), p. 121.
2. George Washington, "Farewell Address," *The World's Best Orations*, Vol. X, ed. David J. Brewer (Akron, Ohio: The Werner Company, 1899), p. 3749
3. Thomas Chalmers, "The Use of Living," *The World's Best Orations*, Vol. III, ed. David J. Brewer (Akron, Ohio: The Werner Company, 1899), p. 1025.

Index